The
CHANGING
ROOM

Change Your Mind. Change Your Life.

JOE GREEN

For permission requests, contact:

Quiet Storm Publishing

Phoenix, Arizona

www.joegreenspeaks.com

ISBN: 979-8-9998830-2-5 (paperback)
ISBN: 979-8-9998830-1-8 (eBook)

Cover design by Jennifer Federico Stimson

Interior Formatting by Melissa Williams Design

Edited by Lisa Daily

Disclaimer: This book is intended to inspire, encourage, and support personal growth and mindset transformation. It is offered for informational and motivational purposes only and is not intended to replace professional advice, diagnosis, or treatment from a qualified mental health, medical, or other licensed professional. The author and publisher disclaim any liability arising directly or indirectly from the use of the information contained within. Readers are encouraged to take full responsibility for their own choices, well-being, and personal development.

Published by Quiet Storm Publishing

Be Heard. Feel Seen.

ACKNOWLEDGMENT

A special thank-you to my dearest friend Leah, who walked beside me every step of the way, offering unwavering love and support. Your love was the peak from which I took flight—and the place where I came to rest when I needed it most. This book exists because of you.

ACKNOWLEDGEMENTS

DEDICATION

For every soul ready to step into the changing room—to release the old, embrace the new, and rediscover their power within. I'm with you every step of the way.

Table of Contents

CHAPTER 1

Own the Moment

*When you pause to stand in the present,
you reclaim your power to begin again.*

You already know there's a greater version of your life waiting.

You can feel it—a quiet but undeniable call to evolve, to step forward, to become your best self.

But somewhere along the way, life got heavy, responsibilities piled up, sacrifices were made and doubts crept in.

The days blurred together, and the bigger dreams grew quieter.

Maybe you've tried before, only to get overwhelmed or distracted.

Maybe you've carried around silent hopes, but were unsure of how to start, or how to keep going once you did.

Maybe you even started to wonder if real change was just for other people.

Here's the truth...

It's not your fault.

No one showed you how to create sustainable change in a world that constantly demands your time, energy, and attention.

But the good news is, it's absolutely possible.

Best of all, you don't have to do it alone.

This isn't just another book.

The *Changing Room* is your pathway to personal growth, powerful change, and a practical space for true transformation.

Inside, you'll find:

- Real-world encouragement that meets you where you are without judgment.
- Transformational insights that awaken clarity, confidence, and new motivation.
- Valuable insights along with daily affirmations—a supportive, powerful approach to help you move from stuck to unstoppable.

You'll also discover how to:

- Break free from old habits, fears, and mental roadblocks.
- Build daily momentum with small, meaningful actions.
- Strengthen your confidence, clarity, and emotional resilience.
- Create your own sustainable blueprint for deep, meaningful change in your life.

I understand what it's like to stand at the crossroads of wanting more, yet feeling unsure about how to move forward.

You feel stuck.

But it doesn't have to stay that way.

Feeling stuck is not a setback; it's a sign that you've outgrown where you are and it's time to move forward.

This book is intended to help you discover a clear, compassionate path forward that honors your pace, your possibilities, your purpose, and need for more.

Now it's your turn.

It's time to feel good again—about yourself, your choices, your future . . . and so much more.

Over the past three decades, I've helped people from all walks of life rebuild confidence, find their direction, and design the lives they were meant to live.

I want the same for you.

You can do this and you don't have to wait until everything feels perfect to begin.

This is your chance to reconnect with your truth, rewrite your routine, and reimagine what's possible.

I'm so glad you're here.

You've made a powerful choice by choosing this book.

Let the journey begin.

CHAPTER 2

Creating Space for Change

True transformation begins when you make room for it—in your mind, your day, and your heart.

Change doesn't require a dramatic overhaul or perfect conditions.

It asks for presence.

Intention.

A pause in your day to return to yourself.

That's why I created this book around the idea of a Private Changing Room, a space that belongs entirely to you.

While it's not a physical room, though it can be, it is more about creating a mental and emotional space where you check in with yourself and get in touch with what you really need in life right now.

This chapter is here to help you bring the idea of The Changing Room to life, to turn it into a real, repeatable part of your week, and ideally your life.

Think of it as your personal check-in point, a place where you press pause, take a deep breath, and intentionally reset.

What Exactly is Your Private Changing Room?

Imagine walking into a peaceful space—no expectations, no noise, no judgment, just a slice of authentic "me-time" where you can try on new thoughts, rejuvenate your mindset and step back into the world just a little clearer, more connected, and more confident.

That's what this is.

It doesn't have to be fancy.

It doesn't require aromatherapy, ocean sounds, or elaborate routines (though you can absolutely include those if you like).

It just needs YOU, showing up for YOU.

It can be:

- A chair in the corner of your bedroom.
- Your parked car with the radio off.
- A park bench on your lunch break.
- Your bathroom with the door locked.
- A quiet morning moment before the day begins.
- Maybe a notebook and cup of tea on the back porch.
- The important part is that it feels like it's YOURS.

How to Use This Book and Start Your Private Changing Room Ritual

Don't rush.

Give yourself the time and attention that you need and deserve.

Real transformation often starts with small hinges that swing big doors.

So give yourself the gift of a pace that is patient and supportive.

Here's a simple way to create your own ritual:

Your Changing Room Ritual

Claim Your Space.

Choose a quiet, comfortable place where you can spend at least *16 minutes* without interruption, once a week. Make it feel personal, even if it's temporary. Let it become your sanctuary.

Gather Your Tools.

You will need a pencil and paper or, if you prefer, *The Changing Room Companion Workbook* available online, and a mirror (handheld or full-length).

You will be looking in the mirror to really help focus and connect with yourself.

This is not about your appearance.

It's about the incredible power of seeing yourself, looking into your own eyes and how it gives you that real, honest and literal experience of self-reflection in the physical sense.

Take Time to Reflect.

Start by reading one *reflection* along with its accompanying *daily affirmations*.

Read slowly, allowing the words to settle in. Then pause—sit quietly, and let your mind unwind and the message sink in.

Now, ask yourself what part of what I just read really resonates with me right now, and why. What is the takeaway message for me?

Write It Out.

Then take 5 to 10 minutes to journal freely. Let it all spill onto the page—your reactions, your fears, your ideas, and even your resistance.

This is your safe space.

It's all about you and only you.

Take Action.

Review what you've written and think about the thoughts and feelings that came to mind in that moment. Think about changes you would like to make and create a two-step TrAction plan that you can and will follow over the next 3 to 5 days.

Keep it simple and realistic.

Make it doable.

Let your mind refresh and begin sketching out your unique blueprint for change.

You're creating momentum and this is how it starts.

Sample Suggestion to Support Your Ritual

After reading a reflection passage, take a few moments to think about what you've just read while reviewing the daily affirmations that follow.

Give yourself the time and patience you need to compose one or two thoughtful questions that speak to your current feelings or circumstances. Based upon your thoughts and answers, create a *TrAction Plan* and write at least one new positive affirmation.

These will represent the personal change(s) you will be working on over the next 3 to 5 days.

Here's an example:

Question: "I know I want more out of life, but I keep holding back instead of stepping forward...What's really stopping me?"

TrAction Plan: Choose two simple tasks, one that you already do every day, and one that you normally would not do but would like to. Then plan to do each of these every day over the next five days, and each time, pause and remind yourself, you can do this.

Positive Affirmation *"I can do anything I put my mind to. I have the power, the freedom and the ability to be successful. Success feels good."*

You can write everything down in a notebook, or use the Companion Workbook found online to find even more motivation, guidance, and structure.

Whatever works best for you.

See this through and really give it your all and you will be pleasantly surprised and proud at how your answers and mindset shift over time.

Why This Matters

This ritual isn't about perfection and it's not about "fixing" yourself.

It's about giving yourself room to pause, to realign, and begin again—over and over, as many times as you need.

Consistency beats intensity in the long run.

If you stick with this once a week—over time, the changes will add up.

You will begin to see your needs and desires more clearly.

You will make decisions with more confidence and certainty.

You will better understand what you want and need, and what matters most to you.

That's the quiet, powerful promise of *The Changing Room*.

You don't have to do it alone.

You just have to begin.

As you move through the pages ahead, just know there's a place waiting for you if and when you're ready to go a little further.

It's the ***Continue the Conversation Community***—a dedicated online space I created, where you and others who seek change, can go, and explore things more deeply with extra guidance, journaling inspiration, motivation steps, and a little steady support.

You don't have to do anything more than read this book, but if at some point you feel like continuing the journey, the door will always be open.

Make *The Changing Room* a natural part of your daily routine.

It's your turn.

It's time to feel good again.

I'm so glad you're here.

P.S. I created a free **Changing Room Starter Kit** you can download. It includes a few printable tools to support your next steps—journaling pages, a weekly action plan, and a handful of reflection suggestions.

No pressure.

Just a gentle nudge forward, if and when you're ready.

Visit <u>joegreenspeaks.com/StarterKit</u> to get yours.

It's absolutely FREE.

CHAPTER 3

Discover Your Power Within

The strength you seek has never been missing—only waiting for you to see it.

Welcome to the first step of this exciting journey. No instruction or advice could ever be fully realized without first feeling empowered to take full advantage of it. These reflections are best read in a space, like your private changing room, where you can meet them with openness and focus. Each reflection builds upon the last, guiding you from self-recognition and acceptance to a state of enhanced self-belief, confidence, and control. You'll find practical insights and tools designed to resonate with your personal experiences, empowering you to harness your inner strength and embrace proactive living.

With an open heart and open mind, I invite you to embark on this transformative journey and discover the empowering potential that lies within you.

The following reflections are about:

- Self-belief
- Self-confidence
- Self-control

Embrace Your Unique Self

REFLECTION

"One of a Kind"

"No price is too high to pay for the privilege of owning yourself." —Friedrich Nietzsche

YOU are special.

Don't wait for someone else to make you feel that way. Truth is you have to believe that you are something special before you can even begin to truly experience and appreciate that.

The people around you are meant to fan the flames of the fire that burns within. In other words, your friends and family are here to enhance what already exists inside.

So ask yourself—what are you doing to make yourself feel special?

If you're doing little to nothing at all then you've got to get started and you can by practicing gratitude for what you have and who you are.

Be grateful for everything and take nothing for granted.

You have arms, legs, toes, your health, your talents.

You have the ability to love, to share, to forgive, to accept, to try again, or to start something new.

That's SPECIAL.

You might be a friend, mentor, role model, parent, sibling, coworker, relationship partner, an inspiration to others, and so much more.

The depth of what you mean to others will not always be known or even understood. You just have to trust that your purpose is absolute and that your presence is enough without validation.

Everyone has what it takes to be a blessing to someone else and everyone will help someone else in some way because it is the circle of life.

Do not focus on what you are NOT.

Doing so only encourages sadness and a lack of gratitude and appreciation for the true value of how special you really are.

Understanding the fact that you are special is not a form of conceit. While it may be construed as such, it is truly the foundation from which all good things grow—self-esteem, self-confidence, self-awareness and the beauty and power of selflessness itself.

Remember . . .

You are special, you always have been and you always will be.

You help make the world a special place just by being in it.

You are one of a kind and your imperfections are your specialties.

There is no greater value than that of your own self-worth.

Share your special brand of love, laughter, and kindness by just being you because somewhere, somehow, it's exactly what someone else needs.

This reflection is the message that you needed to hear.

It's the reminder that you need to think about.

Accept it and embrace it so that the light within you can shine brightly wherever you go.

Read this and pass it on. Chances are someone, somewhere, needs to be reminded of how special they really are, too.

DAILY AFFIRMATIONS:

"I am proud of myself and that is all the validation I need."

*"I practice gratitude everyday by expressing
thanks for everything in my life."*

"It feels good to share the best of what I have to offer."

"Embrace All the Parts of You"

"To keep the body in good health is a duty, otherwise, we shall not be able to keep our mind strong and clear." —Unknown

Before you lace up your sneakers and resolve to start anew, read this reflection.

Good health is an absolute privilege that should never be taken for granted.

Your health impacts you and everyone around you—your family, friends, co-workers, neighbors, and even your pets.

In fact, the quality of your health is a significant part of why you feel the way you do. It contributes to your thoughts and connects to the decisions that you make daily.

Making the decision to be healthy and happy involves taking care of yourself. You have to like yourself enough to give your mind, body, and soul exactly what it needs. In other words, embrace all the parts of you.

You deserve it!

Understand your strengths and use those strengths to improve upon your weaknesses.

As the saying goes, "Good, better, best never rest until your good is better and your better becomes your very best." Remember, humility sacrifices the need for recognition in exchange for the blessings of real rewards.

What would make you a better version of your former self?

Practice healthy habits of living by establishing a higher purpose that truly resonates with you. Exercising and eating healthy really have no merit until you can connect to those goals with passion and emotion.

In the film *Rocky*, the character battles his way back to victory in his matches because he connects to a higher purpose, one greater than winning. He does it for those that he loves in his life.

What's your higher purpose?

Position yourself for success by gaining clarity about what you need versus what you want.

The process of determining the difference between your needs versus your desires gets you halfway to where you should be, and knowing the difference opens the door to success.

Will you give yourself the permission you need to succeed?

The pursuit of accomplishing a healthy lifestyle that affords you all the benefits of a healthy mind, body, and soul starts from within and manifests itself for the outside world to see.

DAILY AFFIRMATIONS:

"I am worthy of love."

"I deserve to have what I want."

"I accept and embrace every part of myself."

Cultivate Self-Acceptance
& Validation

REFLECTION

"Validation"

"When you realize how much you're worth, you'll stop giving people discounts." —*Karen Salmansohn*

Your value is immeasurable.

In most cases you will probably never know exactly how much you mean to others.

Some will tell you, a few might express it, and others will fail to show you any signs of affirmation.

In fact, some may even take you for granted and others may try to bring you down, hoping that you will doubt yourself as they do themselves.

Regardless, you really don't need anyone to validate you or your self-worth.

The greatest appreciation you will ever know is your own appreciation of yourself.

How you feel and how you perceive yourself is one of the most powerful and impactive images that your mind's eye will ever see and capture.

Validate yourself by humbly appreciating and accepting who you are as you are.

Remember that the only person who can truly validate you is you. It's really all about what you think and believe.

It's about the acceptance of self in recognition of the fact that you are essential, that you are special, and that no one can take that away from you.

The right people will appreciate what you have to offer. They will see the best in you, and when you understand this, you will come to realize just how wonderful you really are.

There is no need to force anything, no need to impress or prove yourself.

Just being yourself is enough for those who truly enjoy the light of your existence.

DAILY AFFIRMATIONS:

"I am enough."

"All I need is within me."

"I know that I am special and I choose to treat myself like the valuable person that I am."

"Love Naturally"

"Of all the relationships you will ever have, the most committed and longest lasting of them is the one that you have with yourself." —L.A. Green

Love is first born within and is something that you eventually practice toward yourself.

The way you love yourself helps you discover and understand how you want and need to be loved in relationships with others.

Once you realize you need not search nor wait for love, knowing that you attract what *you* are, who you are, and how you are in a naturally wonderful way—then that yields exactly who and what you need when the time is right.

Love then is as it should be, free of finite definition and as individualistic as every person capable of it, subject only to the interpretation of those who choose to celebrate it within, without or with another.

Regardless of its roots, chosen or allowed, given or received love is resilient and grows when it is planted in the right relationship.

Nourishing that love begins from within; it seeks the light of another with whom to share, and it blossoms in blooms of joy and happiness.

Therefore, the ultimate practice of love happens when you choose to help another love themselves so much so that it becomes a love shared by you and enough for two.

That, my friend, is love naturally.

DAILY AFFIRMATIONS:

"I love myself unconditionally."

"I am giving the love I deserve in return."

*"I am beautiful from the inside out and today
I choose to let my love light shine."*

Harness Inner Strength
& Personal Power

"Walk in Your True Power"

"Your thoughts are the architect of your destiny." —David O. McKay

It is estimated that the typical person has between 60,000 to 70,000 thoughts during the course of a full day, every single day.

Out of those thoughts, 90% are the same as the day before.

So if your thoughts impact your life and the experiences in it, then it stands to reason that the same thoughts always lead to the same choices.

Those same choices lead to the same attitudes and responses, which in turn, drive the same feelings and emotions that connect to the exact same thoughts.

It's a cycle that repeats itself over and over again.

Because the way that you think, act, and feel are all a part of your personality, which is the manifestation of your own personal reality.

Truth is, if you understood just how powerful your thoughts are, you would take better care of your thoughts when you're alone and even better care when choosing the words you speak.

You can do this.

You can start using the power of your mind to bring the peace and joy that you want in your life.

Start with these 5 daily practices:

Pay attention to your conscience.

Listen to the voice inside. When faced with doubt, work on your interpretation of what that means. Replace resignation with exploring your vast imagination.

Pay attention to your behaviors.

Your responses are the reflections of your feelings and experiences from the past. See challenges and moments of uncertainty as opportunities to create a new and different outcome, one that you desire.

Pay attention to your habits.

Separate what you do from who you are. Good or bad, what you have done in the past does not define you; it only describes you and the journey of steps that it took to get to where you are today. You have the power to change the future.

Pay attention to emotions.

Feelings spark responses. Examine both the cause as well as the effect that situations have on you to better understand how to manage and change the end results in your favor. Whatever you feel happens only with your permission.

Pay attention to your words.

Be careful about what you say. It's not just others who are listening, you are too. Your mind, body, and spirit are always listening. Speak as though every word will come true.

Remember that the power of what you're thinking is a legitimate force that contains the power of making things happen.

Using the power of your mind includes creative thinking, imaginative questioning, research and contemplation, envisioning yourself achieving your goals and the expectation to succeed because you believe.

So start now.

Don't leave this life wishing what you should or could have done.

Instead, bless your life and everyone in this world with your ideas, your talents, and your gifts.

You owe it to yourself.

Don't you think?!

DAILY AFFIRMATIONS:

"I trust my instincts and the gift of my natural intelligence to guide my actions and decisions."

"I choose to not only learn from my mistakes, I will make them count by reflecting on what I can do to improve."

"I promise to take chances, to start over again and again, and begin doing the things that I keep putting off."

"The Power of Being Yourself"

"Who you really are is really all that you have to offer." —TQS

Who are you?

I really wanna' know!

Don't you?

That question just happens to be the name of a song from an old rock and roll band named "The Who." The song, like the name of their band, asks the question, "Who are you?"

Are you certain of who you are, or has a situation or experience given you reason to reconsider and ponder the answer?

Understanding who you are gives rise to the opportunity of harnessing the incredible power and potential that you truly have within you.

So often we overlook, underrate, and sometimes even dismiss the talents and gifts that we have, and when we do, we not only cheat ourselves, we rob the world and deny those we call family and friends of the benefits.

The power of you just being you is immeasurable. You may never know, never hear, ever see, or fully understand the impact you have in this world. You don't have to be a star or a famous icon to affect the lives of others.

Just be YOU.

Choosing to be your authentic self is not about someone else liking you. It's not about being accepted or embraced by others. Those things you must do for yourself.

Taking advantage of the power of being yourself starts by looking within yourself and working your way out. This is the process of self-evolution, the work that never ends.

Self-evolution starts with liking yourself enough to spend time enriching your mind with ways to improve your thoughts and opinions. It includes loving yourself enough to put in the time and energy needed to really take good care of your mind, body, and soul on a regular basis.

As you evolve, you will come to embrace and accept yourself in a more meaningful and deeper way by finding ways to become a better version of your former self.

When I was last asked if I was still the same person I used to be, I smiled, and replied, "I sure hope not. I work every single day on being a better friend, father, partner, coach, speaker, listener, communicator . . . you name it, I'm working on it."

My own personal self-evolution continues on, as everyone's should—not because of failure but because there is no such thing as perfection, only progress. Becoming a better person requires self-awareness and reflection.

Here's a great way to get started on becoming a better version of your former self:

Self-evolution TrAction Steps

Write down 5 things that describe who you are.

Rate each from 1-10 (1 = Not so good, 5 = Pretty good and 10 = Excellent) along with just a few words to explain why.

Write down the date you wrote this and put it out of sight, somewhere safe.

Revisit this list in exactly 90 days (set a reminder in your phone).

Day 90, retrieve the list and review it.

Jot down today's date and rate yourself again on each of the 5 things that describe you. Be sure to note if there have been any changes, any progress, or setbacks along the way.

Repeat this exercise and add a "can-do" list. This list is composed of things you can and will do to help improve and continue to progress.

Do this for each of the five things that describe you.

Remember, it's about progress and taking it day by day.

The best part about working within is that it removes the worry and waste of energy wishing and waiting for something great to happen to you.

Keep doing the work, good things are on the way!

DAILY AFFIRMATIONS:

"I give to myself so that I have something valuable to give to those I love—my all."

"Being my authentic self is enough for me and for those who truly love me and care about me."

"I am grateful for what I have and who I am."

Prioritize Personal Well-Being

REFLECTION

"Choose You"

Be kind to your body, gentle with your mind, and patient with your heart. Stay true to your spirit, cherish your soul and never doubt yourself." —Becca Lee

What do you see when you look in the mirror at yourself?

What is your opinion of the person you see in the mirror?

Just like the image in the mirror that moves whenever and wherever you move, so too do your thoughts and the words you speak guide and impact the direction in which you move through life.

As you speak, so you listen.

As you listen, so you think.

As you think, so you believe.

As you believe, so you are.

Your body is listening to your thoughts and your mind is recording your internal dialogue, ingesting every detail.

This is how you come to form an opinion about yourself.

Even though you have the power and opportunity to change your mind at any time, that power is often forgotten and replaced with self-sabotaging thoughts and false beliefs.

When that happens, it hurts you.

It diminishes you and your hopes and dreams.

But it doesn't have to be that way.

You can have the job you want, the kind of relationships you want, and more, by taking a sincere interest in yourself.

It's TRUE and . . .

It starts by choosing YOU.

Understanding yourself is not always easy to do, but if you take the time to self-reflect and question yourself, you will quickly discover what it takes to make yourself happy.

You deserve to give yourself the same friendship, love, and understanding that you give to others.

Depending on others to make you happy is like waiting for the wind to blow before you exhale.

Start taking care of yourself now.

Follow these steps to get started:

Find out if you're being human or if you're just hardly being.

There is a difference.

Take a moment to reflect and evaluate just how human you're really being to yourself.

Are you . . .

Being kind to yourself?

Being forgiving of yourself?

Being accepting of yourself?

Being supportive of yourself?

Being confident in yourself?

Being patient with yourself?

Being honest with yourself?

Being gentle with yourself?

Being a best friend to yourself?

Start being more kind, forgiving, supportive, patient, and honest with yourself.

Remember you've got to be okay on your own before you can truly be okay with somebody else.

Repeat these steps for the rest of your life.

Because as Rupi Kaur once said, "How you love yourself is how you teach others to love you."

Be the example and be the solution to yourself, for yourself and . . .

Choose YOU!

DAILY AFFIRMATIONS:

"The relationship that needs the majority of my time and attention is the one I have with myself—I'm all in."

"I believe in the power of words whether they are spoken or just thoughts coming to mind. I control the narrative."

"I can't expect to put myself last, give myself nothing, and still expect to get exactly what I want in return."

REFLECTION

"Worthy Is a Mindset"

"Your value doesn't decrease based on someone's inability to see your worth." —*Zig Ziglar*

What's really holding you back?

You might be wondering the same thing. Whether you realize it or not, you might be stuck. Maybe you're stuck in a boring career, or you're in an unhappy relationship that's run its course, or you're just flat-out frustrated because you need a jump-start, something to get you going again.

It's okay, we all get stuck at one time or another. It's a part of life. But the key to getting what you need to get yourself moving forward again starts with these important choices:

Choose to . . .

Recognize it. Acknowledge there is an issue. Honor the fact that you have needs. Shed the guilt and stand in the truth. Get everything out into the light and let the sun shine in. This is an important step because it allows you to understand how to help yourself and it gives someone else the insight they need to help you if you decide to reach out for help. This is the first step in reclaiming your power and strength.

Choose to . . .

Address it. Talk about it and get it out. Start with some internal dialogue and chat with yourself about it. This is particularly powerful when you're honest and open with yourself. The results are even more POWERFUL when you look in the mirror at yourself, maintain eye contact, and speak aloud to the image in the mirror that is staring back at you. Don't underestimate this experience. Give it a chance. It's a great way to gain the perspective and clarity that you need. It's worth it and it really works.

Choose to ...

Take action. Reach out to a friend you can trust, or better yet, hire a life coach or counselor to help you successfully navigate your way through your dilemma. This will help position you for success much sooner than later.

While contemplating the best course of action, grab a pen and paper and list 3 actionable steps that you can take right now.

The steps you'll take are instrumental in making one of the most important decisions that you will ever make in life—the decision to open your mind.

When your mind is open, possibilities arise, and if you allow it, the excitement of the potential outcome of those possibilities fills the air with hope and optimism.

For many, this is very difficult, especially when you're used to entertaining sabotaging thoughts that lead you to believe that failure is imminent or that you're not good enough.

You have to break that cycle and smash those thoughts by replacing them with a new attitude.

You have the power.

It may not be easy, but then again, most things that are truly worthwhile in life require you to fight for it.

WORTHY is a MINDSET.

When you make the shift and decide to change your mind, you gain the amazing power to change your life and everything in it.

Say it until you feel it.

Think about it until you believe it.

Picture it and dream about it until you see it.

"I AM WORTHY."

You are indeed worthy of success, good fortune, love, and whatever your heart desires.

You just have to believe.

I believe in you!

DAILY AFFIRMATIONS:

"I refuse to allow guilt or shame to steal my voice."

"I promise to break patterns of silence and speak my truth without apology."

*"I see differences in opinion as a chance to learn
and enhance my personal perspective."*

Develop Self-Control & Decision Making

REFLECTION

"For Peace Within"

*"Rather than being your thoughts and emotions,
be the awareness of them."* —Eckhart Tolle

Gaining self-control often involves taking a step back, reflecting, and slowing down the thought process so as to think rationally and with less emotion.

Sometimes it's hard to balance your thoughts and emotions. Workplace conflicts, relationship challenges, inner turmoil, illness, and financial stress can all wreak havoc on your state of mind and your ability to remain calm, cool, and collected.

It takes a lot of self-control.

Easy to say, but even harder to do because the art of self-control is multi-faceted. It takes applied effort and a lot of practice.

These steps will help you increase your self-control especially when you need it most.

Practice these tips:

Use the slow-motion catch.

Catch the challenge in slow motion. In other words, deal with the challenge at hand in your way, on your time, and at your pace.

Don't be afraid to walk away and process your thoughts and feelings in private. Let that incoming call go to voicemail; read that email or text message when the time is right (when you're ready). Slow things down and allow yourself to have the time and space that you need.

Look at the big picture.

Analyze all of the possibilities and really think things through openly and honestly. Reflect on what transpired and work on answering one of the most important questions of all . . .

WHY?

Remember, solutions solve problems and problems need answers, so use your time and energy wisely.

Avoid the major pitfalls of raw emotions.

Never make decisions when you're extremely tired, very upset, or intoxicated. This is a recipe for regret. Be at your best so that you can decide what is truly best for you. Make decisions that you're proud to take ownership of, ones that demonstrate true self-respect.

Prioritize your rise.

Get rid of the head trash by eliminating irrational thoughts in exchange for focusing on how you can prosper, how you can not only rise above but also benefit from the experience that you are faced with. There's always a way up and, as difficult as it may be, let nothing block you from climbing to the top, above all the hurt, blame, and shame.

Remember, you can influence far more than what you can control around you. So look within yourself to discover what you really can and should control in your life.

That's the art of self-control

DAILY AFFIRMATIONS:

Repeat these daily affirmations to practice your own self-control

"I inhale positive energy and exhale fear."

"I release things that are out of my control."

"I am not afraid of the unknown because I choose faith over fear."

"Move Away from Temptations"

"What lies in our power to do, lies in our power not to do." —Aristotle

Temptation is something that everyone faces; it's a natural part of life.

Whether it's a craving for a sweet treat late at night or a decision in another aspect of your life, the choice is yours.

Like the quote above says, you have the power to do or not to do.

Successfully managing the balance of your thoughts and emotions while you wrestle with temptation requires three important steps.

Name and claim it.

Recognize and acknowledge that you not only have the power to choose but that you also have the responsibility to claim the consequences.

This approach is a very powerful influence in the process of making good decisions where temptations exist.

Think about it.

If you could not speak and your decision were to stand alone without explanation, how would it sound?

I choose to _____.

Steer clear.

Search for the right solution with the goal of finding a successful resolution.

The right solution is one that makes you proud of yourself because you know that it is the right choice to make.

Mistakes are just mistakes until they are repeated or finally defeated.

Think about it.

If you could only write down your decision without any explanation, how would it sound?

I choose to _____.

Practice your peace.

What you do once in a while takes a while, while habits happen often.

Strength in every step you take increases with consistency. Proof of that is the effort that it takes to break a habit.

Grow strong day by day.

Repeat these steps, reaffirm your choice, and revisit your reasons for making the decision that you made.

Think about it.

If you could only demonstrate your decision without words, what would that look like?

It looks like you chose to _____.

So the next time temptation comes along, see it for what is.

Temptation is the itch that signals the need for change.

Make the right changes and you won't have to think about how it looks or how it sounds with or without words.

Because a sound decision stands on its own merits.

DAILY AFFIRMATIONS:

*"Seeing things as they really are is the kind of honesty
that will help me grow in every aspect of my life."*

*"I recognize temptation as a need to reflect and discover
the necessary changes that I need to make."*

"I am going to make time to do something that brings me peace today."

REFLECTION

"Suit Yourself"

"When outfitted with the truth, it's much easier to suit yourself." —TQS

Are you living the life you imagined for yourself?

Once you discover the amazing power that you have to write the story of your life, you will soon realize the importance of each and every day for the chapter that it is, as it unfolds and reveals the story of your life's journey. Every moment is a page recorded and preserved, needing only the power of a decision to turn the page to the next moment in time.

Making the decision to live your life in a way that satisfies you and makes you happy is not only important, it is essential. In fact, you will need to make several decisions in different areas of your life to experience true happiness.

When you think about the decisions you've made in the past, ask yourself...

Do my decisions accurately represent me?

Do my decisions promote my values?

Do my decisions serve me and my purpose for living, loving, and for striving to be even better than I was yesterday?

The answers to these questions tell a lot about your ability to experience and enjoy real happiness.

Your decisions are powerful expressions that represent your innermost thoughts and feelings. Making the decision to enjoy your life to the fullest is a conscious choice that only you can make.

But you have to be open and honest with yourself, because the friends you choose, the partner you share your life with, the job you have, and the material things that you purchase can only stimulate the happiness that already exists inside of you.

You have the power and choice to choose happiness, to choose forgiveness, to accept peace and love in your life, and so much more.

It's your CHOICE.

Making the decisions that need to be made in order to reach the level of happiness, peace, and contentment that you want in your life will inevitably require some changes.

Some of those changes may be tough and even scary, but they're well worth it.

As you approach this process, pay attention to your thoughts and feelings. Recognize the difference between the decision itself and fear of the outcome. There's a difference, and it's usually fear of the outcome that makes the decision-making process so tough.

Focus and rise above your fears. When you do, it will significantly diminish uncertainty and relieve tension and anxiety.

Try these TrAction steps to sharpen your decision-making powers:

Exchange compromise for patience.

Replace fear with wisdom.

Resist negativity with optimism.

Denounce doubt; choose determination.

Embrace challenge to discover change.

When I started to practice these decision-making powers on a regular basis, I experienced an amazing shift.

I could feel it in every fiber of my being that my life was getting better the day I began to assume nothing—the moment I decided to do more, the minute I started to require less, the day I chose to smile more often, the times I turned disappointments into the courage to dream big, and the second I vowed to laugh freely and recognize how blessed I truly am.

I made mindful decisions that I knew would serve me—choices that reflected my values and aligned with my purpose in life. And I continue to make those choices every single day.

Those choices stand on their own merits, without description or further explanation, and they give me the power and confidence I need for everything else.

Remember, what's right for you isn't always what's right for everyone else, and that's exactly what makes your decisions unique and perfect for you.

Decide with your eyes wide open.

Live well, and choose the content for the narrative of your personal life story, because ultimately, the choice is yours.

DAILY AFFIRMATIONS:

"I am committed to making the kind of choices that represent my true character, without a word spoken."

"I choose to evolve and become the person I want to be."

"Deciding what is best for me is already inside of me, just waiting to be discovered."

Empower Personal Growth & Willpower

"The Power of Permission"

"Give yourself permission to pause to create sacred space, the space to consciously choose how you want to respond to any situation." —Dr. Debra Reble

What I am about to say, everyone knows and can understand, but yet the question remains: Are you ready to hear the truth and follow the path that you must travel to get to a better place, to get where you're going, to get where you want to be?

If you answered yes, and you're reading this right now, then I believe you have desire. I believe you're ready to move on to better times and that you're ready to make strides toward your own personal, professional, and life goals.

No matter what your goals are (health and wellness, fitness, nutrition, relationship management, professional performance, recovery), what I am about to share with you really works. And it all starts as soon as you give yourself full permission for serious and meaningful change to happen to you.

You have to allow yourself to be successful.

You have to give yourself permission to succeed.

Think it's easy? It's not.

Things like ...

Self-imposed doubt, low self-esteem, lack of confidence, fear of success, lack of support, a negative attitude, a minimalist mindset, fear of failure, and bad habits are examples of things that make the seemingly simple task of giving yourself the power to receive the permission you need to succeed not only hard but virtually impossible.

When you feel that way, your thoughts follow, your actions follow, and soon without even realizing it, you become a believer. Belief molds you like clay in skilled hands, shaping every thought, every choice, every part of your being until it is inseparable from who you are.

It consumes you!

So let me ask, what's your PERMISSION BLOCKER?

In other words, what's holding you back? What's really stopping you from getting ahead, from reaching your goals?

This is an important question and the answer is even more important because identifying the problem gives rise to the opportunity to fix it. It's the difference between standing still and moving ahead.

But first, you have to know what is holding you back, because the unknown is the resting place of fear, and fear holds you still; it takes away your vision and sabotages your thoughts.

Let's take a closer look:

Fear holds you in place. When you're scared, you're still because you're not sure when or where or even what your next move should be.

Fear takes away your vision. When you're afraid, you imagine the worst of the worst and you see terrible things happening.

Fear sabotages your thoughts. You start thinking about what will happen and how it will feel as your mind runs wild with crazy possibilities and visions of negative outcomes.

You must ERASE the unknown and eliminate fear by identifying your permission blocker, because your permission blocker *is* your fear. They are one and the same.

Once you know what it is, then you can deal with it, break it down, and conquer it. Then you can start to process it by thinking about it, talking about it, and, at some point, reaching out for help if you need it.

You might seek help through life coaching, counseling, or support groups. Whatever you choose, take that next step by getting some help.

YOU'RE WORTH IT!

Let me say that again. That should not be taken lightly. Because it's true and I know that some people have never heard that said to them before, or at best they haven't heard it told to them in quite a long time.

YOU'RE WORTH IT!

Your dreams are worth it, your feelings are worth it and now it's up to you to do the work that has to be done.

Remember, the road to success begins in the mind, resonates in the heart, and then it shows up in the words we speak and in the actions we take.

Mind, body, spirit . . .

You have the power!

DAILY AFFIRMATIONS:

"I give myself permission to feel the way I do so that I can better understand what my needs are."

"I am worthy of permission to have a second chance."

"I allow myself to embrace my strengths and weaknesses equally and humbly."

"The Power of Will"

"Our attitude toward life determines life's attitude toward us." – John Mitchell

The power of will is the power of positivity, and it can work for you personally and professionally.

Using the power of will is the art of choosing your words and arranging your thoughts in a way that illuminates the positive even when the message is not favorable.

The power of will is not a matter of saying yes to everything, nor is it being overly enthusiastic.

The power of will is different from willpower. Willpower is an act of determination, discipline, and perseverance.

The power of will is a communication style that becomes a skill. It is the art of communicating positivity in a very subtle but effective way.

I recall working in the insurance industry, where I occasionally faced the dreaded task of telling someone that their claim was not covered—not exactly good news.

Because I eliminated negative words and focused on solutions, these potentially heated conversations often ended with the person thanking me and expressing appreciation for how the discussion was handled.

I developed a deliberate approach to these conversations: I eliminated negative words, focused on solutions, and maintained a positive tone. Even when the news wasn't good, the person on the other end often thanked me for the clarity and appreciated how the discussion was handled.

It was the power of will.

When asked if a claim for damages was covered, I spoke positively, eliminating negative words such as can't, won't, or don't from the conversation. I focused instead on solutions—ideas to mitigate the damage or reduce additional costs.

This communication style delivers honesty with a hint of positivity: courtesy, practical solutions, and an extra step that leaves the door open to possibility—even when the chances are slim.

Positive conversations feel good for everyone involved. People want to be heard, taken seriously, and respected, and empathy goes a long way in making that happen.

Rather than saying what you cannot do, focus on what you can do. Replace negative words like no, won't, can't, and never with constructive alternatives.

Of course, there is still a place for a well-timed "nope" or "no way"—used sparingly, these words carry more weight.

Because negativity has become automatic in many interactions, your words have the power to stand out. Let them smile as loudly as your voice.

Use the power of will with friends, family, co-workers, and customers alike, and watch the seamless transition take hold—positivity becomes the norm, and conversations transform.

At its best, the power of will . . .

Verbally embraces the other person.

Makes the other person/people feel heard and valued.

Gives the impression that you care and understand.

Helps infuse positivity into a negative experience.

Leaves everyone feeling positive in more ways than one at the conclusion of the conversation.

You can use the power of will when you answer a question, or decide to make a necessary change, or even relay unfortunate news.

The power of will is about what you can do; it's about the effort you will make; it's about the positive, even in a negative situation.

The power of will is POSITIVITY at its best.

DAILY AFFIRMATIONS:

"I am bringing a can-do attitude to everything I do regardless of the challenges I face."

"I am committed to offering and explaining what I can do."

"I am using the power of will to stay focused on the positive."

Enhance Coping Skills & Patience

"Coping Skills"

"Success is not final. Failure is not fatal. It is the courage to continue that counts." —Winston Churchill

Everyone has a canvas to work with . . .

It's LIFE.

Your life is your canvas, your decisions are the colors that you choose to work with, and your attitudes are the variety of the shades of those colors.

Whatever you choose to make of your life is influenced by your ability to cope with life's challenges as they arise and learn from them after they pass.

How you deal with loss, handle relationship issues, process disappointment, and manage personal health challenges is all connected to your ability to cope.

But coping isn't easy, so it's important to remember that even the toughest of times are not only inevitable, they're necessary.

Because it's the hard times that keep you coloring inside the lines of your canvas.

The tougher the times, the greater the focus you need.

You will also find that as you begin to focus, the lines that were once blurred with distress will sharpen from the brushstrokes of a clear and honest applied perspective.

The mere practice of tirelessly searching for perspective in the worst of situations is in and of itself very powerful, because perspective is the majority of what coping skills are made of.

Coping skills are a blend of what it takes to get by, to manage and make it through, to heal and move on.

Coping is a process that unfolds one step at a time, in measured steps, until the balance of your conscious and subconscious mind is restored.

It truly is the ebb and flow of life.

But you have to choose the skills for coping that work best for you and practice by consciously using them regardless of how minor or major the situation is.

Here's a great way to practice coping while using the kind of perspective that moves away from staying stuck in turmoil and gravitates toward resolution.

Honor and accept the fact that . . .

It's okay to make mistakes.

It's okay to ask for help.

It's okay to be afraid.

It's okay to not always be okay.

It's okay to start over as many times as needed.

Shift your mindset and remind yourself that . . .

You are stronger than you think.

You can handle this.

You just have to slow down and breathe.

You will give yourself all the time you need.

You are grateful for the good in your life.

You honor and acknowledge your feelings.

You are not defined by your anxieties.

Trust in the power of the mind for it believes what it sees, it listens to everything it hears, and it sticks to whatever you choose to believe.

Choose your skills and cope wisely.

DAILY AFFIRMATIONS:

"I don't have to entertain negative thoughts. I have the power to change my mind."

"Fears are obstacles to overcome, not the end."

"It's okay; I don't have to have the answers to begin coping with my stress."

"The Power of Patience"

"Patience is not the ability to wait. Patience is to be calm no matter what happens, constantly take action to turn it into positive growth opportunities, and have faith to believe that it will all work out in the end while you are waiting." —Roy T. Bennett

It's hard to wait, especially when you're excited, angry, or depressed. No matter how many quotes you read or movies you see where the hero prevails after a lengthy struggle, the fact is, it's hard to be patient.

Patience is a practice.

These actions lend themselves to practicing the art of being patient.

Think before you speak.

Take time to be alone.

Refocus daily.

Employ faith.

Move step by step.

Patience is a requirement.

You have to believe in what you want.

Attract what you want (Be it).

Reach for what you want (See it).

Feel what you want (Imagine it).

Remember what you want (Think it).

Hold on to what you want (Never give up).

Patience is a language.

Patience is something that speaks volumes about you, for you, and to you.

Patience says you are committed to whatever it is you want.

Patience tells a lot about the depth of your desire.

Patience explains the value and importance of the goal or event.

Patience speaks to others in their own language, telling them all that they need to know.

Patience silently communicates the unspoken truth about your inner strength.

Patience shapes your moral character by removing rash reactions, replacing impulsive behaviors, and by eliminating regretful results.

Respect the process.

Be patient with yourself first and foremost. Accept the highs and lows of practicing patience until the highs and lows become one and the same. When this happens, your focus sharpens and your path to success straightens as you approach your final destination.

Wishing you the power of patience in your life and all of the wonderful blessings that flow from it.

DAILY AFFIRMATIONS:

"I trust that everything will happen exactly when it is supposed to."

"I prefer the ease of patience over the angst of impulse."

*"I am practicing patience so that I can enjoy the
serenity of peaceful moments as they arise."*

Encourage Action &
Personal Responsibility

REFLECTION

"Own the Moment"

*"There is no passion to be found playing small,
in settling for a life that is less than the one you
are capable of living." —Nelson Mandela*

Call it energy, strength, motivation, attitude, spirit, drive, power...

Those are all great buzz words that are often presented as traits to strive for.

I remember the first time my life changed in a major way. I was in my early twenties. I was involved in a serious near-fatal car accident. A school bus rear-ended my car and rode up over the passenger-side roof, practically crushing that side of the car to the ground.

I can still remember the crunching sound of the impact, the engine of the bus, and the chards of flying glass hitting the back of my head and neck like it was yesterday.

I was lucky to get out alive.

Painful rehabilitation followed in an attempt to mend the injuries. After several months of therapy, I met with my doctor to discuss my progress and my new normal going forward.

He came into the exam room, closed the door, and sat down. After a series of questions and a few basic tests he looked at me and said, "Your insurance will not continue to cover the therapy you need. You have two choices. You can deal with life as is and I can prescribe something for your pain or you can continue the therapy exercises on your own and work on trying to get stronger ... It's up to you."

I was scared, I was in pain, and I could barely imagine trying to get stronger on my own. But after a few moments of silence, I looked up, fought back my tears, and told the doctor that I would skip the pain meds and pass on settling for a partial recovery.

I decided to try to get stronger by continuing to exercise on my own.

MOMENT defined!

I went on to recover well beyond the initial prognosis. In fact, I pushed my recovery to the limit. I not only got stronger, I took back my health and the life I thought I might have lost.

You can do this too.

Whether it's at work, in a relationship, or in any situation where a decision is needed, the power is in your hands. Moving forward is a choice, and you have the capability to shape the outcome. It all comes down to believing in that choice—and in yourself.

Try it—own the moment and make a decision.

Have faith in yourself and waste no time looking back, for history is static and only that which you have now, the *present,* is fluid.

Don't settle for a life that is less than you are ultimately capable of living and enjoying.

And remember, it's not the fall that matters, it's the decision to get back up that really counts the most.

TRUST YOURSELF!

DAILY AFFIRMATIONS:

"I recognize something inside of me that wants more and I'm going to get it."

"The moment when everything changes starts with a decision and my mind is made up."

"I'm taking my chances because they're mine to take—I control the chances and I own the moment."

"Greatness"

"Perfection is not attainable, but if we chase perfection we can catch excellence." —Vince Lombardi

A friend shared a message from a historical quote that reminds us that perfect is the enemy of done.

As focused as you may be, the pursuit for perfection is often a distraction. The best use of your time and energy rests in structure and consistency.

To reach your full potential, it's essential to focus on two critical elements of growth: structure and consistency.

Structure

Reaching your full potential doesn't happen without organization, which is the single most important contributor to your overall success in life.

Prioritize, strategize, and synergize your efforts and goals on a regular basis so that your focus becomes singular and your results inevitable.

One mind, one plan, and one approach is the footprint of structure.

Remember the goal of organization is to promote clarity for the sake of simplification—seeing things for what they really are.

Consistency

Success is never guaranteed, but the promise is that if you try again and again, progress becomes inevitable.

Consistency is the engine that drives results. By showing up, day after day, with deliberate focus and effort, you reinforce habits, build momentum, and create lasting change.

You can be GREAT on purpose.

Leave your signature wherever you go and with everyone you meet—strangers, good friends, and casual acquaintances alike, because the impression you make is carried with them.

Be goal-oriented. Be relentless in your approach every day, because each day represents a new opportunity for growth, for success, and for surpassing your previous best.

Be that powerfully positive "force of nature" that radiates warmth, energy, and possibility.

Fill the cup of others.

It's hard to be anything less than successful when you commit to being the best you can possibly be.

When you do, it affects the people around you. The more time we spend together, the greater the impact we have on one another.

Be GREAT at being a friend, a spouse, an employee—and in any other role you choose.

Because YOU CAN BE.

You just have to want to.

DAILY AFFIRMATIONS:

"Today I organize my thoughts, my feelings, and intentions by prioritizing and planning what I will get done."

"Hard work works but consistency wins."

"Regardless of any setbacks or compromises required, success is mine."

CHAPTER 4

Transform Through Action

Small, consistent steps turn intention into reality.

Every person reaches a point where change is no longer just an option—it becomes a necessity. That realization has brought you here, to the most important step: making the decision to accept and implement change.

When you come to understand the true power of change and what it can do for you, you begin to see its value in many areas of your life. This step in the journey invites you to explore themes of self-evolution and personal growth while also facing the very real challenges of fear and obstacles along the way.

As we move forward together, you'll discover the essence of change is more than transformation—it is the key to growth, resilience, and lasting success. As you read on, you'll find a practical and integrated path forward, filled with tips, tools, and reflections designed to help you commit to growth, navigate transitions, and embrace adaptability in times of uncertainty.

You will also learn how cultivating hope, setting healthy boundaries, and finding your true place in the world can nurture self-compassion and ultimately open the door to forgiveness.

Embrace this part of the journey, and allow yourself to experience the transformative power that lies within change.

The reflections in this section are about:

- Self-Evolution
- Personal Growth
- Facing Fears, and Challenges

Initiating Change & Embracing New Beginnings

"You Need a Fresh Start"

"The secret to a rich life is to have more beginnings than endings." —Dave Weinbaum

You've been getting the chance of a lifetime since the day you were born.

You get the chance to start all over every time tomorrow turns into today.

That's amazing and pretty powerful too.

Because that means you can do just about anything. You can change your mind, set new goals, start something new, forgive, believe, quit, or make up your mind to try again.

Many people squander their chances; others retreat in fear from the chance to start over, citing a lack of time and energy as the reasons why they're just "hanging in there."

But hanging in there isn't always good enough.

You know that and that's why you need something more.

Sometimes that realization doesn't make its way to the forefront of your mind until it becomes painfully obvious.

But that's okay because the first step in starting over is to realize that it must be done.

The next step is accepting that realization and the third step is the action step...

Embracing it (aka Taking Action).

The difference between settling for what is and reaching for what could be is born in the decision to start living the rest of your life instead of dying toward what's left of your life to live.

So stand up right now.

Inhale the longest, deepest breath of air that you possibly can and then exhale very slowly.

Don't rush the steady, smooth flow of air leaving your lungs—that's the feeling of old energy releasing and new energy taking its place.

It's REFRESHING.

Now it's time to organize the process of starting over.

Start with reflection.

Take a good look at your daily routine, your habits, weaknesses, and strengths. Then measure what you discovered against your true desire and potential and be honest with yourself. Then identify the changes you need to make.

Clarify your intentions.

Simply put, establish what you want and what you need to do to be happy, to feel fulfilled, to be the best version of yourself going forward. Create a plan to refresh your approach and get started today.

Commit to change.

Once you've looked within and defined what it takes for a healthy, successful new start, make the decision to stick with it. Apply these three steps to every area of your life where a fresh start is needed.

No change is too minor and no chance is too big to pass on if it's really worth it to you.

Need help mustering the courage to hit the reset button? Talk to others who have successfully started over. Or research and read up on ideas on how you can start over in your particular situation.

Remember, you're just as deserving as a pro athlete or actor, of having a professional coach.

The real risk and the greatest loss both exist in failing to start over when starting fresh and new is exactly what is needed.

Like a rose bush, prune now and then watch your dreams grow into something beautiful in the future.

DAILY AFFIRMATIONS:

*"I am very fortunate to have the gift of another day—
this is my chance to start over and try again."*

"Starting over is the opportunity to improve."

"The best way to move on is to start over."

REFLECTION
"Wake Up"

"If you want to make your dreams come true the first thing you have to do is wake up." —J.M. Powers

This reflection was inspired by a true story.

An elderly woman who lived alone suffered a stroke one day and collapsed on her floor. For several hours, she lay there helpless until a neighbor discovered her and called for help.

She was rushed to the hospital but didn't recover as well as she had hoped. In fact, she was told she would never fully recover—that she would never get better.

Feeling defeated and written off, she spent her days in a nursing home bed, losing hope with each passing day.

Then, one day, her son found a specialist who focused on post-stroke rehabilitation and arranged for him to work with her. She shared her story—her frustration, her disappointment, and her longing for a chance to prove them wrong.

Little by little, things began to change. First, her fingers twitched. Then her hand moved. Soon, her arm and leg began to respond. It was as if her body were waking up from a deep sleep—and so was her spirit.

Her progress was remarkable. The nursing staff, her doctor, and her son were all amazed. She grew stronger, got out of bed, and began to look forward to the future again.

Her mind, body, and soul had been reawakened to new possibilities.

She was truly rejuvenated.

Everyone faces moments in life that feel hopeless. Sometimes, it's hard to reignite that fighting spirit—especially when the odds seem stacked against you.

When you're feeling overwhelmed, the best way to rejuvenate and recover is to begin by reestablishing the mindset that anything is possible.

Start by waking up your imagination. Picture the success you want to experience and the resources you need to make it happen. If you can see it in your mind, you've already begun to create it.

Let your imagination run free—don't restrict it with doubt or fear.

Once you've revived that spark of determination, take action. Do your homework. Search for what you need and refuse to give up until you find it.

Like the elderly woman who suffered a stroke, look beyond the challenges. Stand on top of your setbacks to gain a clearer view of what's next and how to move forward. Her persistence and her belief that recovery was still possible changed everything.

You can do this too. Wake up your imagination. Begin your search for the guidance, support, or opportunity that will help you move ahead.

Keep trying, even when progress feels slow. Breakthroughs often come right after the moment you're tempted to stop.

When you want something deeply enough, you'll find a way to make it happen—because nothing less will satisfy you.

So wake up. Open your eyes and the mind behind them—to all that's waiting for you.

DAILY AFFIRMATIONS:

"I can. I will."

"I'm putting it out there and making it known that I am leaving the door open to possibilities—to receiving everything and anything, from something great to unbelievably fantastic."

"I am allowed to want more for myself."

Confronting & Overcoming Fears

"Live Fearlessly"

"Always remember you are braver than you believe, stronger than you seem, and smarter than you think." —Christopher Robin

Living fearless doesn't mean being free of fear. It means living fully in spite of it—reaching for your greatest potential, loving with your whole heart, failing big, trying harder, and holding on when it would be easier to let go.

It's about giving your all.

Today, break up with fear and leave behind limiting beliefs, past mistakes, and sabotaging thoughts.

Until you release them, you'll remain captive—waiting for the perfect time, the perfect day, the perfect version of yourself that doesn't exist.

Start a new relationship with yourself by choosing to live your best life now.

What does living fearless look like?

Live in and for the moment.

There are only three days in your life: yesterday and tomorrow—neither of which you can change or control—and today, which is all you truly have to work with.

Choose honesty and seek the truth.

Be honest with yourself about yourself. No one knows you better than you do, and no one else can make the changes that only you can make.

Replace excuses with plans.

The best-laid plans are meant to evolve. Growth comes from progress, not perfection.

Practice humility through accountability.

The humble heart accepts responsibility. The humble mind learns from it.

Love yourself enough to trust yourself enough—and so it shall be.

Living fearless isn't about eliminating fear—it's about rising above it. Each time you face what scares you and move forward anyway, you prove that courage was within you all along.

Fear less. Live more. Trust your strength and keep moving forward.

DAILY AFFIRMATIONS:

"Today I am making the decision to be free."

"I inhale confidence and exhale fear."

"I am in charge of my life, no one else gets to have that power."

REFLECTION

"Pride Aside"

"Pride is spiritual cancer, it eats up the very possibility of love, or contentment, or even common sense." —C. Lewis

Protecting yourself from life's greatest harms is an inherent responsibility.

Yet hurt and disappointment will surely arise along the way.

Those are the inevitables.

They are the emotional experiences that make us both human and capable of loving and being loved.

But sometimes it's foolish pride that gets in the way of experiencing all of the best that life has to offer.

A better day, an easier way or a return to the simplicity of peace and joy in life can become more complicated and harder to achieve than it has to be.

But it doesn't have to be that way.

You can change all of that by putting ego driven pride aside.

Apologize first instead of waiting, admit to your shortcomings and accept them as a chance to grow and look for opportunities to be a better version of your former self.

Reinvent yourself.

To achieve something you've never had, you must be willing to do something you've never done. In that process, you'll inevitably reinvent yourself—that's what first times are all about. They're the moments that shape something new, and someone new: you.

Remember, whatever holds you molds you—so choose to rest only in what serves you best.

"Whatever holds me molds me, and I alone choose what that will be."

"My soul knows the way; I am making the decision to follow."

"I give myself permission to start over."

Commitment to Personal Transformation

"Way to Be"

"Your life does not get better by chance; it gets better by change." —*Jim Rohn*

Be something you've never been before.

Be early instead of late. Be happy instead of sad. Be the first to offer an apology instead of waiting to receive one.

Be fearless.

Be disciplined.

Be kind.

Be empathetic.

Be the person you would love to count on. Be the best friend you've ever had. Be the one who loves you the way you want—and need—to be loved.

Be that person for yourself first, so you can share that same experience and those same feelings with someone else.

Becoming who you want to be takes real commitment and the willingness to change.

It's possible and here's how to get started:

Five Ways to Reinvent Yourself

Set Goals.

Decide exactly what you want and focus on it. The first step to achieving anything is clearly seeing it.

Break big goals into smaller ones that guide you toward your ultimate vision.

Plan to succeed—knowing that even if your reach is a stretch, the results will be worth holding onto.

Leave Your Comfort Zone

Everything worthwhile lies on the other side of challenge. Get up, get out, and get going. Change is the recipe for success. As intimidating as it may feel, it's equally rewarding.

Remember, self-evolution is a continuous journey, not a final destination.

Speak Your Truth—Assertively

Mean what you say and say what you mean. Words carry power, and their impact is shaped by intention. Speak from the heart, and your message won't just be heard—it will resonate.

When your actions align with your words, confusion disappears and trust grows.

Take Daily Action Toward Authenticity

Find your true north. Get in touch with yourself and rediscover what brings you peace, love, and happiness.

Eat healthy. Exercise regularly. Stretch daily. Meditate often. Unwind more. Laugh freely.

Always remember to breathe.

It's not what you do once in a while that turns dreams into reality—it's what you do consistently that creates lasting success.

One day at a time is all you have. One foot in front of the other is as fast as you can go. One moment at a time is all you need.

Support your true self.

Refresh Your Circle of Trust

Review and renew every relationship, including the one with yourself.

Release situations and people who no longer align with your goals for peace, love, and happiness.

Create a reality worth living—and the way forward will reveal itself.

Yes, you can.

DAILY AFFIRMATIONS:

"My possibilities are endless."

"I know I have to give to myself in order to justify expectations of getting what I want in return."

"Self-evolution is a journey not a destination. That's why everyday, I am on my way."

REFLECTION

"Fast Forward"

"You are allowed to be both a masterpiece and a work in progress simultaneously." —Sophia Bush

Have you ever wondered why you feel the way you do?

Where does the very essence of you come from?

The truth is, much of who you are today stems from learned behaviors and early life experiences—many formed when you were just a child.

It's no mystery why you think and feel the way you do now; those patterns have been hard-wired from your most humble beginnings. Your childhood shaped more of who you are than you probably realize.

What you were taught and the experiences that molded you growing up, continue to influence your life in this very moment. Wise advice, rules and consequences, family traditions, beliefs, and daily habits have all contributed to how and why you think, feel, and act as an adult.

What you carry from childhood into adulthood shows up in your relationships with others and with yourself. It shapes your attitudes, behaviors, and the choices you make every day.

Recognizing this is incredibly powerful because it not only explains a lot, it gives you clarity and direction. That understanding helps you recognize what needs attention and how to work through challenges as they arise.

Remember, growth requires awareness. You can't create meaningful change until you understand what needs to change. That means taking inventory of your personal history—acknowledging where you've been while keeping your eyes on where you want to go.

When you begin connecting your most impressionable years to the present, your capacity to understand yourself and to be understood by others expands by leaps and bounds.

We all carry "our stuff" with us—our emotional baggage—into this daily event we call life.

How you handle that depends on three things:

Your Recognition

Take your own pulse. Notice what you're feeling and explore the reasons behind it. Often, the cause runs deeper than what's visible on the surface.

Your Understanding

Get honest with yourself. Be raw and vulnerable as you search for the real reasons behind your emotions.

Your Management

Once you've recognized and understood what's happening, create a plan to address it. Communicate openly if conflict arises. Trace your feelings to their source and work toward resolution.

Ask for help if you need it. Most people do, because growth is rarely achieved alone. Self-evolution is one of life's most rewarding pursuits. The journey of continuous personal growth, of breaking through limitations and embracing your full potential, is both your education and your achievement.

Start today with these Five TrAction Steps to become a better version of your former self:

REFLECT

Take an honest, unfiltered look at yourself. Consider what makes you who you are and why.

RECOGNIZE

Seek out opportunities for new challenges and experiences that can reshape how you think, feel, and live.

REINVENT

Your thoughts and words shape how you see yourself, as well as how others see you.

Replace limiting beliefs with empowering ones. Speak positively, even when it feels difficult.

For example:

"I can give this a try. I'm capable of learning."

"This may be stressful, but it's an opportunity to grow."

REFOCUS

Every day brings a fresh start and a new chance to move closer to your goals. Choose at least one action daily that supports your growth.

At day's end, review your progress, then refocus for tomorrow.

REALIGN

Choose your circle wisely. Surround yourself with people who uplift and inspire you—those who share your desire to grow and evolve.

Replace negativity and distractions with positivity and purpose

Here's a powerful way to bring these five steps to life right now:

Write a letter to your future self.

Describe in detail the person you want to become.

Outline the greatest challenges you expect to face and how you plan to overcome them.

Identify the most limiting belief you hold about yourself and rewrite it as a positive affirmation.

Then, describe your strategy for success and note who or what you'll release to clear away negative energy—and what or who you'll invite in to replace it with positivity.

End your letter with this promise:

"I'm on my way, and I promise, I am worth the wait."

Practice these steps daily. Like anything worthwhile, consistency is the secret sauce that brings lasting change.

You've got this.

DAILY AFFIRMATIONS:

"I won't run and i vow to no longer hide from the truth and the hard work that needs to be done."

"I know that I am ready for change because the way things are now just isn't good enough anymore."

"It's time, it's my turn—here I come."

REFLECTION

"What's Next"

"We must be willing to let go of the life we planned so as to have the life that is waiting for us." —J. Campbell

What are you going to do next?

Sometimes the next chapter of your life arrives unexpectedly—without warning, planning, or invitation. Other times, it feels like a long journey toward an unknown destination.

Figuring out what comes next is more than an exercise of free will; it's a search, a deep dive for answers that don't always reveal themselves as quickly or clearly as you'd like.

Maybe you're contemplating a career change, moving to a new home, starting a new relationship, transitioning into retirement, or stepping into a new role—like becoming a grandparent.

Whatever it is, you'll need to process both your thoughts and emotions. In doing so, you'll need five essential perspectives.

First, You'll Need Patience

Decisions about your future take time—and rightly so. The choices you make now are the ones that shape how you experience life ahead.

If you're reading this, chances are you're not just searching for what's next; you're seeking something meaningful and fulfilling.

Search with patience to find what fills your cup. The results will be worth the wait.

Second, You'll Need Some Alone Time

Let the wisdom of your years rise to the surface. Your past experiences, lessons learned, and deepest desires reveal themselves when you take time to truly reflect.

You can't hear your inner voice if you're constantly surrounded by noise.

There's a time and place for everything—find yours. Quiet your mind, and the distractions will begin to settle.

Sometimes you simply need space to just be—to show up and be there for yourself.

Third, You'll Need Honesty

You'll always fall short of what you really want if you compromise the truth.

Be honest with yourself about what you want and what you need.

While doing so, release judgment and fear. Give yourself permission to explore every thought and possibility that comes to mind.

You must be honest with yourself in order to be your best self.

Almost-truths come in shades; honesty shines in full color.

You deserve the truth from yourself just as much as you do from others.

Next, You'll Need Vulnerability

It's not always easy to open up as much as you need to.

Low confidence, self-doubt, uncertainty, and fear of outside opinions can all stand in your way.

But where vulnerability exists, opportunities arrive.

Finally, You'll Need Courage

Finding the answers is only half the journey.

You must believe in yourself.

Believe that you are worthy. Believe that you are capable. Believe that you are strong.

Most importantly, believe that whatever it is you want can be yours—and that if you truly want it, it already is.

Courage is claiming what you desire so you can attract what's next into your life.

When you finally figure out what's next, remember: it's not about the past—it's about what lies ahead.

It's about being present, grounded, and in touch with who you are today.

You're not who you once were—and you shouldn't be. You're meant to evolve, to grow into a better version of your former self.

Discovering who and what you've become is what the present is all about.

Open the gift of today and find out . . .

What's next?

DAILY AFFIRMATIONS:

"I know that if I can see what I want then it's already mine."

"I am claiming the courage I need to go after what I want."

"I am on my way to becoming the best I've ever been."

"Live Your Life on Purpose"

*"Your purpose in life is to find your true self
and express it authentically."* —*Lao Tzu*

Do you feel content—or do you want more out of life and your relationships?

The truth is, your ability to get what you want, and what you need to feel happy and fulfilled, all comes down to one thing: taking care of business.

Taking care of business means taking care of yourself so that you can live and enjoy your best life.

Whether you realize it or not, you're already in business for yourself.

You're in the business of living life. And much like a business owner, you are ultimately responsible for your own successes and setbacks.

You have to make important decisions, invest wisely, research, communicate, negotiate, compromise, reevaluate, change, and take action when needed to achieve success.

The same holds true in life, but it's not always easy. In fact, it can be downright scary at times.

Making the most of what you have requires a real investment of time, energy, effort, and consistency.

That can feel overwhelming. But here's the good news:

You're the boss.

Now it's time to step into that role and start thinking and acting like one.

Start by categorizing the major areas of your life:

Health: Mind, Body, and Soul

Relationships: Self, Family, and Friends

Spirituality: Beliefs and Practices

Finance: Personal and Professional

Next, rate and review each area:

Look at the past and present. Add names, titles, and short descriptions where relevant, along with one or two sentences describing your current status.

Examples:

Health: Mind – Always thinking about work and what needs to be done. Feeling stressed and mentally exhausted.

Health: Body – Need to exercise more and eat healthier. This needs to move to the top of my priority list.

Health: Soul – My only "downtime" is when I'm sick. I need at least one daily ritual that helps me feel centered—maybe listening to a favorite podcast each morning.

Do the same for Relationships, Spirituality, and Finance.

Lastly, set Clear Intentions

Write down one thing you should do, one thing you will do, and at least one expectation for each area.

Example:

Health – I should exercise regularly and eat more fruits and veggies.

I will walk after work and add one fruit or veggie to my lunch every day.

I expect this to be a challenge, but I also expect to do it consistently, Monday through Friday, without fail.

Then, add a realistic timeline:

"I will start within the next two days, no later, and stick with it for 21 days. Then I'll review my progress to see what's working and what can improve." Now you're back in business.

You're no longer waiting to see what happens to you—you're creating what happens for you.

Because now you have structure.

You have clarity.

You have a renewed sense of purpose.

Living life on purpose is the surest way to get the most out of it.

If you want to call the shots, you must know where to aim.

Because if you're not living your life on purpose, then even the accidents are on purpose.

You'll find the contentment you seek and a deep sense of peace by appreciating life's experiences in this way.

Let today be the first of many days filled with excitement, clarity, and confidence about where you're headed.

You deserve this.

DAILY AFFIRMATIONS:

"I am on my way to a better day, and nothing can stop my momentum!"

"Winners never quit. I give my best every day, and I keep reaching higher!"

*"Mistakes are my stepping stones—I use them
to soar toward exactly what I want!"*

Enhancing Change & Adaptability

"Keep the Change"

"The only person you are destined to become is the person you decide to be." —Ralph Waldo Emerson

What's new? What's exciting? What is there to look forward to?

It's CHANGE.

Nothing stays the same, that much is a given. But the real message is about seeing change for what it brings to life.

What does not change does not grow, whether it's a plant, a job, or a relationship. Without change, there's nothing new, nothing exciting, and very little to look forward to.

Yet for many, change is dreaded.

Sometimes it feels like a setback.

Sometimes it paralyzes.

Fear of the unknown often keeps people from taking action. Change can feel scary because it brings uncertainty, doubt, and hesitation.

So what separates those who embrace change from those who resist it?

It's PERSPECTIVE.

Seeing change as a pathway to new opportunities isn't always easy—but it doesn't have to be hard for you.

Try this approach:

Greet change with optimism.

Focus on the positives it can bring.

You might meet a new best friend, or even a soul mate. You might find yourself in a better place at the perfect time. You could land your dream job, discover the ideal place to live, or experience something you've only ever imagined.

See change as opportunity.

With it comes excitement and endless possibilities.

Anything could happen.

Try a new trainer or a new diet, and you might finally get the body you've always wanted. Go to a different coffee shop, or step inside instead of using the drive-thru, and you could meet someone who changes your life, just as you change theirs.

Move to a new neighborhood or a new state, start fresh, meet new people, and re-energize yourself.

The possibilities are limitless.

Change by choice.

Don't let change always catch you off guard. You have the power to change whatever you want, your entire life, or just a small part of it, simply by changing your mind.

Think it, and so it shall be.

Instead of letting change happen to you, happen back to change.

Be proactive instead of reactive. Embrace it, don't fear it.

As Sheryl Crow said, "A Change Would Do You Good."

DAILY AFFIRMATIONS:

"When I change, the world around me changes too."

"I grow and improve every day, showing the world the change I want to see."

"I choose to change. I choose to smile, and I choose to live fully."

"The Rhythm of Life"

"Be willing to transition at every stage of your life. If your heart is open and you have an open mind, the blessing will flow." —*T.D. Jakes*

Transition is the bridge between today and the future of tomorrow.

As scary as it may seem at times, making transitions is a natural part of life, something you cannot avoid.

Whether we resist it or embrace it, change is unavoidable.

Resistance often arises from fear of the unknown, false assumptions, or self-imposed feelings of insecurity.

Are you worried about working for a new boss, meeting someone new, growing older, making a tough decision in a relationship, or adjusting to life after the kids go off to college?

These moments will come, and even when you've anticipated them, they can feel bigger than you are—like more than you can handle.

But they're not.

You have what it takes to adjust, to adapt, to flex, and to reshape your routine into a new normal.

To make that happen, you need to do two things.

Reflect and Refresh Your Perspective

Take a step back and examine the changes you're facing. Consider your thoughts and feelings about them, and explore why you feel the way you do.

Ask yourself why, and listen carefully to the answer. The answer may not be the solution itself, but it will shine a light on the real issues behind your struggle.

When you can identify and understand your feelings, you're already halfway toward figuring out what to do next. This is the practice of refreshing your perspective.

Feel it out.

Figure it out.

Talk it out.

Work through it until you can smooth it out.

Revisit Your Intentions and Practice Acceptance

Next, examine your intentions—what is truly on your mind and in your heart, so you can develop the capacity to accept what is.

Acceptance begins with understanding and becomes powerful when chosen over resistance. It's a hug without arms, a voice without sound, a silent message of love and support.

Acceptance is not submission; it's permission.

Seeking to understand, working to resolve, and asking for clarity are all humble steps that allow you to practice the art of acceptance during a time of transition.

The time you spend processing change is always time well spent, especially when it is devoted to refreshing your perspective and finding meaningful, purposeful ways to balance it with sincere acceptance.When in doubt, find a quiet space where you can reflect, pray, or simply be. Let guidance or whatever you believe in, take the wheel, lead the way, and open your hands to receive the blessings of change.

Use this space to shape your words into gentle, selfless expressions of understanding and gratitude, allowing peace and joy to settle.

Find your way.

You belong.

You are necessary, and you always will be, even if your role has changed.

DAILY AFFIRMATIONS:

"I choose to change on my terms, embracing a new normal with confidence and purpose."

"I am who I am, and I will carry my talents and energy with me wherever I go."

"I am open to good things happening, and that's why I welcome and embrace change."

Cultivating Hope &
Setting Boundaries

"Your Message of Hope"

*"Sometimes we can only find our true direction when
we let the wind of change carry us."* —*Mimi Novic*

Loss is more than just absence; it is the beginning of something new.

As true as that is, it's often hard to focus on the fact that when you lose something, or someone, you weren't ready to be separated from, it's okay.

Whether you have lost self-motivation, something valuable, or someone special, know that you are being guided toward a necessary new normal.

While a fresh start or a new way of living might not have been what you expected, it is exactly what you need.

The key to adjusting your sails and going with the flow requires...

ACCEPTANCE.

The sooner you embrace change, the faster you move away from the past and into the present.

The past is history. The present is where life happens, and it's exactly where you need to be.

But, like anything else, acceptance takes practice.

In honor of that, try processing loss by looking in the mirror and reading this letter to yourself: Hey YOU,

Your hardships and challenges are not the end.

They are the beginning of a new normal.

You're on a journey, and you have been since the day you were born.

Along the way, life happens.

How you manage those happenings is what matters most.

The good, the bad, fear, excitement, anguish, surprise, pain, and the unknown—they all pave the way.

While your path is paved with good intentions, challenges will arise.

Change is not only necessary; it is inevitable.

Your ability to adapt and overcome will sometimes require releasing the old to make room for the new.

A new way, a different day, another path.

Regardless of the circumstances, you are still YOU.

You are still a friend, a sibling, a spouse, a parent, and a presence on this earth with purpose.

YOU are ALIVE ...

Because you are not defined by your hardships; you are forged by them.

From that strength, your NEW NORMAL comes to life.

Sincerely,

There's always hope!

DAILY AFFIRMATIONS:

*"We don't lose people; sometimes paths just
simply change and I accept that."*

"My hardships and challenges do not define me; they help me grow."

*"I accept change because I realize that my time
and attention is needed elsewhere."*

"Draw the Line"

"Healthy boundaries are not walls. They are gates and fences that allow you to enjoy the beauty of your own garden." —Lydia Hall

What's acceptable to you defines the structure of every relationship you have.

Your values, morals, needs, and desires shape those boundaries.

Healthy boundaries aren't optional, they're essential. They show others how to love, respect, and connect with you.

If you want to be treated well, loved for who you are, and valued for your perspective, you must communicate your boundaries clearly and honestly.

Expectation without conversation leads to confusion and disappointment.

So, what are your boundaries?

They should reflect what matters most—your values, your needs, your truth.

Consider writing a personal constitution, your own bill of rights for how you want to live and love.

Once you define it, living by it becomes easier.

For example:

My health is my foundation. I make time to exercise, eat well, and rest so I can show up as the best version of myself, for me and for those I love.

Affirmations like this give structure and accountability to your relationships.

Use them to guide how you connect with friends, family, partners, and even yourself.

Organize the chaos.

Refresh your connections.

Share your boundaries, and invite others to share theirs.

Set the tone.

Draw the line and live by it.

DAILY AFFIRMATIONS:

"I honor my boundaries as an act of self-love and mutual respect."

"It's okay to say no; doing so protects my peace and strengthens my purpose."

"The way I teach others to treat me begins with how I treat myself."

Finding Your Place & Embracing Imperfection

REFLECTION

"Where You Belong"

"Fitting in is about assessing a situation and becoming who you need to be in order to be accepted. Belonging, on the other hand, doesn't require us to change who we are; it requires us to be who we are." —Brene Brown

Read this reflection and really take it in.

Once you do, you'll start seeing your own life through a clearer, more empowering lens.

Maybe you can relate to this.

There was a quiet kid named Nelson who grew up in a tough neighborhood. He decided to try out for a nearby football team. He made the team, but no one really noticed him. Small, soft-spoken, and easily overlooked, he spent most games on the sidelines.

Then one day before practice, the kids were tossing the ball around. The ball rolled Nelson's way, and he took off running. To everyone's surprise, no one could catch him. He was fast—lightning fast.

The coaches watched in disbelief. They had no idea how talented he really was. No one had ever thought to ask about his background in track or how naturally athletic he was.

Soon, another team saw what others had missed. They gave him a real chance, and Nelson thrived. Before long, he made the little league all-star team and finally got to show the world what he was capable of.

The truth is, sometimes the extraordinary in you can't shine until you're in the right environment.

You might be like Nelson—full of potential that's waiting for the right place to unfold.

If you're in a situation that dims your light or limits your growth, it's time to make a change. Go where your gifts are seen, valued, and appreciated.

Because when you're in the right place, you don't just survive, you thrive.

That's where your purpose meets possibility.

That's where your extra turns ordinary into extraordinary.

DAILY AFFIRMATIONS:

"I refuse to hide my potential—I'm ready to shine where my light is seen and celebrated."

"My mission is to attract opportunities and environments that recognize my worth and support my growth."

"I know my worth. When I'm where I truly belong, recognition comes naturally."

REFLECTION

"Tried & True"

The doer alone learneth." —Friedrich Nietzsche

There will be times when you see both your strengths and your short-comings, and that's okay.

It's all worth knowing.

We are not perfection; we are progress.

Growing and evolving.

Failing and succeeding.

Hurting and forgiving.

It's the trying that makes life worthwhile. Because if you're not trying, then, in some meaningful ways, you're not really living. Don't fool yourself into believing you're succeeding if you've stopped trying.

Life is meant to be lived, and living it means taking chances.

Nothing ventured, nothing gained.

Stretch yourself.

Learn something new about who you are and what you're capable of. Taste the many flavors that opportunity has to offer.

You won't love every experience, but you won't dislike every one either. Change it, tweak it, reinvent it, and try again.

It takes courage to try, but the harder the challenge, the greater the reward. There's always something waiting on the other side of effort.

Good or bad, like it or not, every outcome becomes experience, and experience becomes knowledge.

Knowledge gives you power. It allows you to teach, to help, and to share. You learn through your own experiences, and through the wisdom of others who have walked before you.

Take the pressure off by shifting your focus from the outcome to what you'll learn along the way.

That experience becomes your gift, something valuable to share with others.

Because trying teaches you.

You learn the most powerful lessons when you discover something new about yourself.

Never stop learning.

The more you know, the more you have to offer, to those who know you now and to those you've yet to meet.

Remember: it's far better to be worth knowing than to be well-known.

I've tried some things once and others many times, because trying challenges me, strengthens me, and reminds me that I believe in myself.

That's why I try.

Now it's your turn.

Whether it's a new job, a hobby, a move, or a relationship—give it, and yourself, a chance.

Try.

Or, as I like to say ... go for a walk and see where the path leads you.

DAILY AFFIRMATIONS:

"I embrace every opportunity to try, knowing each effort teaches me something valuable about myself."

"I give myself permission to take chances, grow, and stretch beyond my comfort zone."

"Every experience I face strengthens me, expands my knowledge, and increases what I have to offer the world."

Fostering Self-Compassion & Positive Attitudes

"You're Not Alone"

*You cannot be lonely if you like the person
you're alone with. —Wayne Dyer*

The longest relationship you'll ever have is the one you have with yourself.

What you put in is what you get out.

Time, movement, rest, reflection, healthy habits, and self-care are all essential to a strong, fulfilling relationship with yourself.

Many know this, yet too few feel truly at peace within.

Ask yourself: when you look in the mirror, what do you see?

How do you feel?

Awareness is only the first step.

To thrive, you need action.

Here are four TrAction Steps to help you reconnect with yourself:

Connect with your inner self.

Listen! Pay attention to your body and emotions. Your instincts are your guide—honor them.

Set aside a few quiet minutes each day: walk, sit, breathe, reflect.

Break down old barriers.

Let go of regret and forgive yourself. Self-forgiveness is the foundation for moving forward.

You can't grow while holding on to the past.

Refresh your thoughts.

Your mind evolves—your thinking should too.

Outdated perspectives hold you back.

Ask yourself: Are my thoughts serving me?

Are my expectations realistic?

Is it time for a reset?

Start over.

Give yourself permission to begin again.

Become the best version of you.

Change your attitude, habits, and mindset.

Anything is possible when you choose it.

Step into your private "Changing Room," look in the mirror, and say:

I've got your back.

You're safe with me.

I'm with you all the way.

I am a blessing.

I am special, and I am worth it.

I am open to new experiences and ready to receive something great today.

The power isn't in believing it perfectly yet—it's in the intention. Give yourself this energy, and it will come back to you.

You are not alone.

You never were.

You are enough, and you always will be.

DAILY AFFIRMATIONS:

"I believe in myself 100% and that is my super power.

"When doubt arrives and challenges appear, I will rise up."

"The better I get to know myself, the better I like myself."

"It's Your Attitude"

"Your attitude, not your aptitude, will determine your altitude." —Zig Ziglar

Your attitude sets the tone for everything—your thoughts, emotions, actions, and the way you see yourself and the world around you.

It touches almost every part of your life.

Your habits, fears, beliefs, setbacks, successes, and even your perseverance all rise or fall with your attitude.

The good news?

Improving your attitude is a choice.

That means you're in control.

You already have the power to change it whenever you decide to.

It's a lot like building muscle—it takes consistency, patience, and a bit of sweat. But the more you work at it, the stronger it gets. Keep putting your best foot forward, and change will come.

Even when you can't change your situation, you can always change your attitude.

Try these five attitude adjustments to shift your mindset and lift your spirit:

Change what you can in your world.

The way you listen, how you forgive, your daily routine, your health—these are all in your hands. Every small change counts, and remember: change itself is powerful.

Practice gratitude and acceptance.

Start by noticing the blessings in your life and giving thanks for them. Then accept yourself—flaws, quirks, and all, as already enough.

Repeat positive affirmations.

Speak kindly to yourself. Remind yourself that you are good, worthy, and valuable. Look in the mirror every morning and say something positive about yourself, and mean it.

Recognize and manage stress

When stress shows up, don't ignore it. Name it, understand where it's coming from, and take one positive step, however small, to ease it. Don't let it grow; let it go.

Give back to yourself.

Take care of your mind, body, and soul—the three pillars that hold you up. When you do, your thoughts and feelings begin to fall into harmony, and everything just flows better.

Remember, don't just let life happen to you.

Happen back to life.

Because that's the attitude that changes everything.

DAILY AFFIRMATIONS:

"My attitude is the measure of my opportunity."

"I am putting my best foot forward every chance I get,"

"Changing my point of view changes how I arrive at the point."

Embracing Forgiveness
& Moving Forward

"Forgive Your Failures"

"Nobody can bring you peace but yourself."
—Ralph Waldo Emerson

Forgiveness is one of the most powerful forces in life. It's also one of the hardest to reach, but when you do, it's deeply freeing and transformative.

Whether you want forgiveness, need forgiveness, or have the power to give it, you're in a position to grow. No matter where you stand, learning to separate your emotions from your core values and beliefs is essential to finding peace.

Getting to forgiveness is a process.

It takes humility, patience, and courage.

It asks for self-accountability and a genuine desire to understand—not just others, but yourself.

That's where true healing begins.

Ask yourself:

Do you need to come to terms with a regret that still lingers?

Do you need to forgive a coworker's shortcomings so you can stay aligned with your best self?

Do you want to forgive yourself or someone else but just don't know how to begin?

Remember this: forgiveness isn't weakness, it's strength.

It's not surrender, it's freedom.

It takes real courage to forgive when your ego wants to fight back. That inner tug-of-war between pride and peace is where the real work happens. And that's where you have to invest time, patience, and love—for yourself.

Forgiveness isn't just something you give away; it's something you give to yourself. It's an act of self-respect and emotional maturity.

So yes, forgiveness starts with you.

When you choose to forgive, you open the door to new boundaries, healthier connections, and the kind of growth that lets your spirit soar.

Always remember, you are worthy of forgiveness.

Here's a little practice to help you started:

12 Opportunities to Forgive Your Failures

Forgive yourself for how you chose to survive.

Forgive yourself for the desires you judged harshly.

Forgive yourself for spending time on things that didn't fulfill you.

Forgive yourself for pretending to be someone you're not.

Forgive yourself for the ways you expressed pain or frustration.

Forgive yourself for the times you didn't add value to others.

Forgive yourself for what you discovered about yourself that you didn't like.

Forgive yourself for the shortcomings you've seen in yourself.

Forgive yourself for not fixing what you think you should have.

Forgive yourself for not respecting someone else's opinion.

Forgive yourself for holding onto a grudge.

Forgive yourself for not being able to forgive yourself sooner.

Keep in mind, forgiveness is the strength that makes change possible.

It's what fuels growth, renewal, and resilience.

Use it as your tool.

Use it as your freedom.

And above all, use it to move forward and prosper.

DAILY AFFIRMATIONS:

"My relationship with myself matters. I give it the time, care, and energy it deserves for healing, growth, and living my best life."

"I am worthy of a fresh start, every single day."

"I focus on the good within me and celebrate the person I am becoming."

CHAPTER 5

Ignite Your Motivation

When your "why" burns bright, your will can move mountains.

You have arrived. But you didn't come this far to only come this far. Now it's time to begin laying a strong, authentic foundation for change by moving into practical, actionable steps to kickstart your progress.

Here you'll find reflections dedicated to getting started and taking action, that offer insightful guidance on how to initiate the process of transformation.

As you continue, you will discover strategies for pushing past obstacles with perseverance, empowering you to stay the course even when the process feels challenging.

By the time this chapter draws to a close, you will have gained insight into the critical role of consistency and support in sustaining long-term growth.

Together, these reflections will provide you with a roadmap for building momentum, step by step, through action, resilience, and the commitment to keep moving forward.

Embrace motivation as both the spark and the steady flame that fuels your journey: the courage to begin, the discipline to take action, the perseverance to endure, and the consistency to carry you all the way.

These reflections are about:

- Getting started
- Taking action
- Perseverance
- Consistency

Laying the Groundwork for Awakening & Getting Started

"Speak Your Truth"

"Listening is the silent gift that gives peace to those who speak and understanding to those who listen." —Lewis Anthony

Are you having a hard time saying what's on your mind—expressing what's in your heart?

Maybe there's something you need to say, but the timing never feels quite right.

Speaking your truth isn't always easy.

Sometimes, the words just won't come out.

Often it's our own feelings, fears, or assumptions that stand in the way—keeping us from finding the courage to say what needs to be said.

Whether it's good news, bad news, or something uncomfortable, chances are you need to talk it out, especially if it's been sitting heavy on your mind.

Remember this: what you have to say is important and worth hearing, because your feelings matter.

So, how do you get started?

Break down your message.

Take a moment to assess what's really going on.

Clearly identify what needs to be said.

Your message should include what you want, what you think, how you feel, and why.

Hint: *Focus on honesty, not blame. Keep it open, simple, and true.*

Organize your thoughts.

Get to the heart of the matter.

Share your feelings and explain where they're coming from.

Be clear about why you believe what you do.

Hint: *This isn't about defending yourself, it's about expressing yourself*

Get in touch with your emotions.

Ask yourself why this conversation feels hard.

Are you afraid of being misunderstood, rejected, or dismissed?

Hint: *No matter the relationship—friend, spouse, or coworker, if it's worth keeping, the conversation is worth having.* When the moment comes and you have the chance to speak, think first, listen often, and breathe.

Empathize as you go, it helps you stay calm, centered, and open.

Say what you mean, and mean what you say.

Because when you hold back, assumptions fill the silence, and that can change the message entirely.

As Germany Kent once said, "To say nothing is saying something."

So go ahead, speak your truth. You owe it to yourself to be heard.

DAILY AFFIRMATIONS:

"What I have to say matters, my voice has value."

"I choose to speak from the heart."

*"Regardless of how hard the right words are
hard to find, I will speak my truth."*

"Find Your Fire"

*"Sometimes we are tested not to show our weaknesses
but to discover our strengths." —Unknown*

Find your fire—that spark inside you, that innate desire that fuels your drive to succeed.

Whether it's finally standing up for yourself, finding the courage to start something new, or reigniting motivation you thought you'd lost, it all begins the same way.

You have to find your FIRE.

Whatever sets your mind ablaze has the power to spark incredible change and create real transformation in your life.

Now, finding that "get-go" gear isn't always easy—sometimes it feels out of reach.

Believe me, I've seen it, and I've lived it.

Over the years, I've coached thousands of people, most looking to improve their physical health, their confidence, or simply their overall well-being.

Nod your head if this sounds familiar:

"I know what I should do, but for some reason, I'm just not motivated. I can't seem to get going, my heart's only half in it."

You're not alone.

Some people struggle to get started; others struggle to stay motivated once they do. Both are tough, and both require the same thing, honest self-reflection and mindful evaluation.

No ego.

No excuses.

Just you, having a real conversation with yourself.

So, let's get practical.

Here are a few Fire-Starter Tips to help you find (and keep) your fire burning bright:

Clear your plate.

Take inventory of everything on your mind—what you want to do, need to do, and must do, both personally and professionally.

Organize your list by priority and keep it somewhere you'll see it daily.

Get rid of the clutter and ask for help where you can.

Remember, too much is just that ... too much. So take your time, simplify, and start fresh.

Taste success.

Even if you haven't reached your goal yet, you can still experience what success feels like.

Read stories about people who've achieved what you're after.

Absorb their journeys.

Then, instead of comparing, imagine how your story might look.

See it.

Feel it.

Believe it.

Your journey is yours alone, and your reward will be too.

Fan the flames.

Surround yourself with positive people who support your growth and push you forward.

Support matters just as much as energy.

Whether you're driven by encouragement or by the challenge of proving doubters wrong, use what fuels you.

Read uplifting material.

Post affirmations and quotes where you'll see them often.

Join groups, get involved, and immerse yourself in your passion.

Get excited.

Get determined.

Because you have to want it more than anyone else, including those cheering you on.

Positivity burns until success catches fire, and remember: it only takes a spark to start.

Commit to success.

It's one thing to set a goal—it's another to stand up for it and refuse to back down.

Commitment is the heartbeat of success.

It's accountability in action.

When you hold yourself accountable, you're not just committing to the goal, you're committing to you. Because at the end of the day, the only person who can truly let you down ... is yourself.

Commitment means staying in the fight, win, lose, or draw. It means standing back up every time you fall.

Yes, there will be trials and triumphs along the way, but it's your resolve that determines how the story ends.

Some people stop at the pursuit. Others keep going until they reach the finish line.

What makes the difference?

Fire.

Whatever it is that you desire, don't give up.

Keep pushing, keep trying, and keep believing until you ...

Find Your Fire.

DAILY AFFIRMATIONS:

"I stand tall in my purpose, no matter how long the journey is."

"I can't stop thinking about what I want; that's how I know it's worth fighting for."

"I achieve what I believe."

"It's Your Choice"

*"Only put off until tomorrow what you are willing
to die having left undone." —Pablo Picasso*

Don't die with your music still inside you!

Every single day, you face choices, some small, some life-changing.

Making the right decisions for yourself isn't always easy.

Avoidance isn't the answer, even when fear and doubt feel like they've got you in a stranglehold.

Sure, it's wise to pause and reflect, but at some point, a decision has to be made.

Once you make that choice, focus on the how and the why, not on second-guessing yourself.

Yes, hesitation may creep in at first.

Challenges will appear, often when you least expect them.

That's natural.

It's proof you're taking your shot, just like the people who achieve greatness.

Every wrinkle, every scar, every victory and disappointment—these aren't just memories.

They're fuel.

Use them to think, to grow, to move forward—not as shields to hide behind.

That's how you gain clarity.

So if you've been stuck, or paralyzed by indecision, move now.

Take that step.

Remember the incredible power of choice you hold.

Feel it.

Celebrate it.

You get to choose to forgive, it's profoundly freeing.

You get to choose to change, it's transformative.

You get to choose what you believe, and that's evolution in action.

Your choices are your superpower.

Use them wisely, boldly, and without regret.

DAILY AFFIRMATIONS:

"I embrace the gift of choice, and move forward with confidence."

"Where there's a choice there's always a chance for something great."

*"My choices are my lessons and blessings; I am open
and ready to claim them by making a decision."*

Taking Action & Setting Your Journey in Motion

"Chasing Windmills"

"Twenty years from now you will be more disappointed by the things you didn't do than by the ones you did. So throw off the bowlines. Sail away from the safe harbor. Catch the trade winds in your sails. Explore. Dream. Discover." —H. Jackson Brown, Jr.

Are you going through life with your emergency brake on, expecting to get where you want to go and achieve what you truly desire?

Somewhere between what you plan to do and what actually happens lies the story of your life.

You can either take life as it comes, settling for what you get, or you can dream bigger and reach for something more.

Making your dreams come true starts with vision, requires action, and manifests as results.

But you have to go after it. You have to fight for it, wait for it, and never stop reaching for it.

Sometimes, you may even have to start over, more than once.

Remember: your mind shapes your matter. What you think influences what you do, or don't do.

Dreams remain unrealized when fear or quitting take the lead. Breaking those habits starts in the same place where dreams are born: your mind.

One method I use to regain focus and momentum is the *"Slow-Motion Catch Rule."*

It's designed to help you reset your mind and get back in action toward your goals.

When an unexpected distraction or setback occurs, pause for a full 90 seconds (the "catch").

Acknowledge it, then schedule a time at least four hours later to revisit what happened.

This practice lets you take control, turning distractions or disappointments into manageable, solvable issues—on your terms, when you're ready.

Slowing down after the initial reaction is an act of poise and self-control. It may feel challenging, but it's a proven path to success.

The *slow-motion catch rule* works in all areas of life, personal and professional. Whether it's a frustrating message from your boss or an upsetting note from a friend, addressing it when you're physically and mentally ready allows you to rise above the situation.

Yes, it may linger in your mind during the day, and that's okay.

You're processing.

That's the beauty of this approach: it gives you the space to understand how you truly feel, helping you respond in a way that improves the situation rather than making it worse.

Once you've processed, you can move to the next step: talking it over with a trusted resource or addressing the source of frustration directly to find a rational solution.

The best part?

This approach doesn't just serve you, it serves everyone involved.

It encourages reflection, patience, and better communication for all.

Whether or not you choose to implement this rule can be the difference between peace of mind and regret.

To complement this practice, slow down your thought process each morning and read one of the following daily mantras and quotes, then reflect on how they resonate throughout your day:

DAY 1

Mantra: Big or small, today I will take another step forward.

Quote: "Between the great things we cannot do and the small things we will not do, the danger is that we shall do nothing." —Adolph Monod

DAY 2

Mantra: It's my time, it's my turn.

Quote: "Dare to dream, then decide to do." —Annette White

DAY 3

Mantra: I will not settle for less; I deserve more.

Quote: "Don't downgrade your dreams just to fit your reality. Upgrade your conviction to match your destiny." —Stuart W. Scott

DAY 4

Mantra: I can and I will achieve what I want.

Quote: "Dreams come in a size too big so that we may grow into them." —Josie Bisse

DAY 5

Mantra: Yes, I BELIEVE.

Quote: "Not fulfilling your dreams will be a loss to the world, because the world needs everyone's gift—yours and mine." —Barbara Sher

DAY 6

Mantra: It's already done; it's already mine.

Quote: "So many of our dreams at first seem impossible, then they seem improbable, and then, when we summon the will, they soon become inevitable." —Christopher Reeve

DAY 7

Mantra: It must be done.

Quote: "This one step: choosing a goal and sticking to it, changes everything." —Scott Reed

Remember: it's never too late to start chasing your dreams.

You are never too much—or too little—of anything.

Don't give up.

Give your all.

DAILY AFFIRMATIONS:

*"These mantras are my affirmations and they remind me
to take control and move forward, at my own pace."*

*"I choose to live, love, and work at my own pace
because that's what works best for me."*

"Control is mine to lose, and it is also mine to gain."

"For the Life of Me"

"In the end, it's not the years in your life that count;
it's the life in your years" —Edward Stieglitz

What are you going to do with the rest of your life?

Some questions hit you right where it counts, and this one ... well, if nothing else, it makes you really think.

Maybe it brings up some long-suppressed feelings—fear, doubt, or even sheer wonder.

There's no shame in that.

After all, you've probably faced this question before—graduating from high school or college, standing at a crossroads in your career, or navigating a life transition.

I am convinced this is one of the most challenging questions you will ever face.

But why is it so hard?

It's not the pressure to get it right.

It's not that you can't change your mind.

It's not even that you might not know.

It's the opposite.

Figuring out what you want to do with the rest of your life can be overwhelming because of the freedom you have, and the recognition of the abundance of your own power.

The power of your potential is enormous.

You have the ability to choose anything.

To try something new.

To discover hidden talents.

To take a chance.

To start over, again and again, if you need to.

But using that power for your own greater good comes down to taking action in a series of intentional steps that I call *TrAction Steps*.

TrAction Steps are designed to focus your attention and awareness on what you truly want and how to make it happen.

Whether you're deciding what to do after school, navigating retirement, or facing any life transition, the decision is yours.

Try these TrAction Steps to get started:

IDENTIFY

Focus: Break it down: Who are you? Where are you from? Where have you been? What have you done? Why do you need something more or different in your life?

TrAction Step: Discover your next path by asking: Where do you want to go? What will it take to get there? What are you willing to do to make it happen?

RECOGNIZE

Focus: Understand how and why you've made the choices you've made so far.

Where do your feelings stem from—childhood, past relationships, or isolated experiences?

TrAction Step: Finding answers often requires time, patience, and sometimes a trusted, unbiased outside perspective.

Accept the past, but leave it behind—everything you want is ahead of you.

CLARIFY

Focus: Clear the path to new beginnings by understanding yourself on a deeper level.

Be honest, open, and humble—ego has no place here.

TrAction Step: Take inventory: your world, your health, habits, work ethic, attitude toward yourself and others, and your personal values.

Take the appropriate actions to align with your vision.

INTEND

Focus: Move with intention. Live on purpose. Start a new chapter. Be proactive rather than reactive.

TrAction Step: Without change, nothing new happens. Decide to create change and customize it to fit your goals and desired outcome.

INVENT

Focus: By changing your mind, you can change your world. You are exactly who and what you believe yourself to be.

TrAction Step: It's never too late to reinvent yourself. Imagine it, create it, see it, be it—and then believe it.

Who better to write your story than you?

You are the author.

You decide how the story goes. You may need to repeat these steps several times to gain real traction, but it's worth it.

As Mahatma Gandhi said, "Your life is your message."

So ... what's next?

What are you going to do with the rest of your life?

DAILY AFFIRMATIONS:

"I give myself permission to be whatever I want to be, without apology."

"I have the power to reinvent myself anytime I want, and as many times as I choose."

"It's my life, and I am the author of my story."

"Find Your Voice"

"The single biggest problem in communication is the illusion that it has taken place." —George Bernard Shaw

Whether it's an apology left unsaid or the hesitation to express your true thoughts and feelings, chances are you've been on both sides of communication—initiating it or receiving it.

You know how it feels to be excluded or ignored.

You also know how it feels when someone gives you their full attention, listening, sharing, and connecting with you in a way that matters.

That's the heart of communication: to be heard, understood, and ultimately responded to.

The key to creating meaningful communication that truly resonates begins with finding your voice.

Finding your voice starts with understanding your personal communication style.

So, what kind of communicator are you?

Verbal communication works best for those who like to speak their mind and value real-time feedback.

Written communication serves those who prefer to think through their words and express themselves with clarity and care.

Visual communication resonates with those who believe that actions often speak louder than words.

You may have one preferred style, or a blend of several.

Whatever helps you express yourself openly, clearly, and authentically is perfectly right for you.

Practice communicating in ways that feel good and genuine.

Try surprising someone with a compliment, a handwritten note on a sticky pad, or even a cup of coffee.

Every one of those gestures speaks volumes.

Find your voice.

Share your message.

Don't wait—because procrastination is the habit of taking the future for granted.

DAILY AFFIRMATIONS:

*"I speak with confidence, clarity, and purpose—
my voice matters and deserves to be heard."*

"My voice is powerful and I'm going to use it boldly and unapologetically."

*"I only accept healthy relationships where there is giving
and receiving, communicating and listening."*

Overcoming Obstacles, Perseverance, & Resilience

"Follow-Through"

"An ounce of performance is worth pounds of promises." —Mae West

The main reason most people never get what they truly want out of life isn't because they lack talent, time, or opportunity—it's because they're unsure how to go about it.

They stay in pursuit mode, chasing the goal but never quite expecting to reach it.

Whether it's weight loss, breaking a bad habit, improving a relationship, or chasing a lifelong dream—none of it becomes real without one key ingredient: follow-through.

Follow-through is what separates intention from accomplishment.

It's what captures attention, builds trust, and inspires everyone around you.

It matters to children, who believe in what they're told with all their heart.

It matters to leaders, who set the tone for those who follow.

Most importantly, it matters to you.

Because there's no satisfaction in letting yourself down.

True accomplishment—win or lose, succeed or stumble, comes from finishing what you start.

Follow-through builds integrity, honesty, and loyalty. It commands respect and earns belief from those looking for someone to believe in.

Remember this: success isn't fleeting, it's just waiting for you to catch up.

So take a moment and ask yourself these five powerful questions:

Do I know what my end goal is? (Clarity)

Do I know what it takes to reach it? (Knowledge)

How important is it to me to achieve it? (Desire)

What am I willing to do to make it happen? (Intention)

When I get there, what does success look and feel like? (Vision)

Most people stumble on that last question and fall short because they've never taken the time to plan for success.

If you don't know how the story ends ... it never really does.

So today, get up.

Get clear.

Get moving.

Move forward with power, purpose, and conviction ...

Finish what you started.

DAILY AFFIRMATIONS:

"I understand that an important part of seeing things through to the finish includes eliminating negativity in my life."

"I finish strong, no matter how long it takes, because my word, to myself—is my promise."

"I am breaking up with the past so that I can finally live my life through to the finish,"

"Manage the Flow"

*"It's not the load that breaks you down, it's
the way you carry it." —Lou Holtz*

When you place your hand over your heart and take a deep breath, what you're feeling is intention and purpose.

When that rhythm is interrupted—when something disrupts your peace and sense of well-being, that's stress.

Stress is a natural part of life.

We all experience it.

But the real difference lies in how you handle it. Because the way you respond to stress determines the quality of your outlook, your energy, and your results.

Your thoughts and feelings shape how you cope with challenges. The ability to manage them gives you the control you need to ride out any storm.

The stronger your control, the more peace and clarity you'll find, no matter what's happening around you.

Remember, stress is external. It comes from outside of you. But too often, we internalize it. We let it live inside our heads and hearts until it feels like it's part of us.

Bottling up emotions like fear, anxiety, or frustration doesn't protect you, it holds you back from healing, growing, and moving toward higher ground.

Stress is the undoing of your natural desire for peace and happiness.

When you hold on to it, it starts showing up in other ways—short temper, fatigue, distraction, guilt, confusion, even depression.

Sound familiar?

Then it's time to start uncovering the root cause.

Stress often stems from struggles like:

Trying to reach personal or professional goals.

Repairing a damaged relationship.

Overcoming procrastination.

Creating space and time for yourself.

Finding happiness or balance.

Managing money matters.

Navigating health challenges.

Whatever the cause, remember this: a solution always exists.

It begins with one simple act, helping yourself.

So give yourself a helping hand and try these steps now:

Eliminate the "Head Trash."

Free your mind. Choose positive, productive thoughts over sabotaging ones that steal your power.

Replace revenge with repair.

Trade blame for forgiveness.

Focus on finding solutions, not feeding frustration.

Avoid stressful people.

Surround yourself with positivity. Protect your energy by being intentional about who you let in.

Keep company with those who lift you higher and inspire growth.

Distance yourself from stress.

Set boundaries. Give yourself permission to pause. Let that upsetting call go to voicemail, and listen when you're ready.

Handle stress on your terms.

Catch and release.

It's okay to feel it. Feelings are part of being human. But holding on to stress is toxic—it never leads to satisfaction.

Process it, then let it go.

The future is waiting for you.

Make the decision to be free—free to see clearly, to choose wisely, and to act with strength and resolve.

Because the best you have to offer is still ahead of you.

You can conquer any challenge you set your mind to.

You just have to manage the flow.

DAILY AFFIRMATIONS:

"Survivor—that's who I am, and that's what I'm made of."

"My life, my world—I am in charge."

"I am releasing whatever it is that no longer serves me so that I may restore my inner peace."

"Broken"

"Struggle itself is the wrinkled version of success just waiting to be worked out." —TQS

Have you ever asked yourself, "Why me?"

Chances are you have.

Maybe you're having a bad day, dealing with a personal injustice, or coping with regret, or even a chronic illness.

Regardless, sometimes you feel defeated.

Sometimes you feel broken.

It's in these moments the direction you choose sets the tone for what's to come.

Good or bad, action or inaction, the secret to arriving at a better space in life is simple: move forward.

Forward is the direction of progress.

I know this well because my work revolves around helping people move forward.

Why?

Because everything worth having, everything good and possible, is ahead of you, out in front, waiting to be claimed.

That's why moving forward is so important, especially when it's hard, and you don't feel like it.

Forward is the natural progression of life.

I understand both the challenges and the rewards of choosing to move forward, because I choose it every day.

Not because it's easy, or honorable, or even admirable.

I do it because I am alive.

I've been given another day, another chance to start anew.

You have that same incredible power.

Every day you wake up, you get the chance to start over, making the best of the day you've been given.

And along with that chance comes the opportunity to repair what has been broken.

There's no greater work than working on yourself, because the return on that investment is always one hundred percent yours.

Yes, there are many ways you might feel broken.

But here's the TRUTH:

Whatever breaks you ... makes you.

It shapes who you become afterwards.

It makes you stronger, it makes a difference, it makes you a fighter, and it makes you a survivor.

It makes you an example for someone else, because we are all here to help one another.

Remember: some of the strongest leaders, wisest souls, and most experienced experts are who they are because they, too, were once broken.

But they didn't stop there.

They took what was broken, repaired it, and made it bigger, better, faster, stronger. They saw the break for the blessing it truly was, and they marched on.

So how do you begin to repair what's broken?

First, accept that hurt and disappointment are natural parts of life. Everyone experiences them.

Don't feel sorry for yourself—feel your feelings, then start making the necessary repairs.

Look for the lessons hidden in tough times, so you can emerge a stronger, wiser person.

Think ahead, plan ahead, look ahead, and remind yourself: the best is yet to come.

Say it, believe it, and achieve it.

Understand that moving on, feeling better, and trying again are all decisions that start in the mind.

Take time to think, meditate, daydream, or do whatever helps you gently and patiently clear your mind.

Use your superpower: the ability to change your mind. When you do, you can change your life.

As Trent Shelton said, "Never be ashamed about being broken, because strength is nothing but pain that's been repaired."

Be strong, be patient, be well—and keep moving forward.

DAILY AFFIRMATIONS:

"Prioritize the rise."

"I am stronger than my fears."

"I rise and shine by releasing whatever weighs heavily on me."

"Rise Above the Storm"

"Rationality grows well and thrives in the garden of relaxation." —TQS

So long as you are alive, you will always be in pursuit of happiness—recovering from misfortunes, and hopefully learning and growing from your past mistakes.

That's life.

But it's the decisions you make that will either help you or hurt you along the way. Whether it's love or friendship, professional or personal, figuring out what is best for you might just be the greatest challenge of all.

So how do you do that?

What is your process for arriving at a final decision?

Some people turn to a trusted friend.

Others reach out to a coach, mentor, or counselor for guidance.

No matter who you turn to for insight, the greatest wisdom will always come from within—from the one who knows you best . . .

YOU.

But, before seeking answers from the outside world, pause and give yourself space to listen inward.

Because sometimes, the clarity you're searching for has been waiting quietly inside you all along.

Here's a great way to do that:

Stop and Take Time to Reflect

Look within.

Slow down.

Breathe.

Calm your mind with reassurance and presence. This is your moment to pray, meditate, daydream, or simply stretch and let your thoughts unfold.

When you open yourself to all the possibilities that exist, you place yourself directly on the path to clarity, and when you do, the answers you seek will find you.

There's wisdom in waiting and peace in patience.

Trust that what's meant for you will always arrive in its perfect time.

Give Yourself Permission to Release

When you let go, you gain your grip.

As counterintuitive as it sounds, surrendering control often brings the solution into view—be it help, understanding, or a fresh perspective.

Everyone gives and receives help at some point in life. In every exchange, you're either the lesson or the blessing.

Accepting that truth and fully embracing it gives you exactly what you need to find peace and understanding in every situation.

Step Into the Light of Your Own Being

This is where your renewal begins.

Nurture your existence with the conscious decision to reflect and release, so that when the time comes—you can rise above the storm.

Rise knowing you've made peace with what's behind you and, most of all, rise because you're ready to move forward.

DAILY AFFIRMATIONS:

"There's a difference between asking for help and asking for answers—help I need, answers I already have, I just have to figure it out."

"I trust myself to make the right choices, and I have the power to rise above any challenge."

"There are no perfect decisions, just better ones; and those are the ones I strive to make."

Building Consistency & Sustaining Your Momentum

"The Shape of You"

"It's not what we do once in a while that shapes our lives, but what we do consistently." —Tony Robbins

CONSISTENCY is the key to success, and to so much more in life— probably more than you even realize.

This single practice shapes your values, your fears, your faith, your health, your daily decisions, your emotions, behaviors, moods, relationships, and trust—or lack thereof.

It literally impacts everything, yet often goes unnoticed.

To better understand the value of consistency in your life, stop and consider the repeated occurrences that have taken place in your life and how they have impacted you and your decisions.

As you reflect, you will begin to see the connection between consistency and the outcomes you have experienced so far.

You are indeed a collection of your most consistent experiences.

When you come to appreciate that, you will be in a position to put the power of consistency to work for you.

Here's a great way to get started:

GIVE the same time and attention to those you care about every day. Bring the same energy and effort consistently.

Give your all.

When you're consistent, your value is undeniable.

FOCUS on the here and now. Be a source of stability and security by being dependable. Arrive on time, be fully present, and always follow through.

Sometimes your example alone provides the strength someone else needs.

COMMIT to the highest standards in your life. Set daily goals, no matter how small, and take steps toward them every day.

Each step is more than just progress—it's a chance to reach your goals.

It's never too late to be the best son, daughter, friend, boss, student, mentor, or partner you can be.

Your best self is exactly what the world wants and needs from you.

Be your own HERO.

Hard work matters—but consistency rules!

DAILY AFFIRMATIONS:

*"Consistency is my commitment to myself so
that I can be healthier and happier."*

"I promise to do the little things in a more purposeful and meaningful way."

*"I will show up for myself and others with purpose,
discipline, and heart—every single day.*

"Igniting the Inner You"

"Purpose directs passion and passion ignites purpose." —Rhonda Britten

You have it in you—passion, desire, confidence, motivation, success, and so much more.

Yet sometimes you may find yourself in a rut, where nothing seems to spark your interest.

Is it depression, boredom, lack of energy, a need for change, or a blend of them all?

Whatever the cause, finding your way back to a better space and rhythm in daily life is one thing.

But finding that spark is another.

When your heart light goes dim, you'll need to work from the inside out to rekindle the fire within.

Here are a few great ways to do that:

Rub two positives together:

Think of one person or place that makes you smile.

Then think of one blessing in your life.

Allow yourself to fully appreciate both, and feel those positive emotions begin to resonate.

Manage your feelings:

When you're in control of your emotions, your attitude often follows.

Negative thoughts don't have to consume you.

Let them pass through your mind without judgment until they lose energy and eventually fade away.

Connect with your source:

Identify what brings you genuine joy and fuels your spirit.

It could be a quiet moment alone, your favorite music, a special person, or your faith—or a combination of these.

Be patient with yourself.

Don't rush the process, because the process is the fire and your actions are the air that fans the flame.

Go within to seek the light.

Once it's lit, the path back will reveal itself.

DAILY AFFIRMATIONS:

"I'm going to give myself as many chances as it takes to get where I am going."

"No more waiting, I am taking charge and living my best life."

"The beginning and the end are just that, so I'm going to give my all to the process in between."

"Will Power"

"Cogito ergo sum" or "I think, therefore, I am". —Rene Descartes

True story...

A widowed woman once learned of a personal trainer who worked with clients in the privacy of their own homes. She met with the trainer and decided to give it a try.

They quickly hit it off and soon became dear friends. Before long, she came to think of the trainer as part of her family.

Years passed, and she began to struggle with directions, memory, and familiar tasks. She was entering the early stages of Alzheimer's disease.

As her condition progressed, the trainer continued to visit her faithfully, even after she was moved into a nursing home.

During those visits, she rarely remembered much beyond the fact that they were close. So, each time they met, they reminisced as though it were the first time.

She was delighted, and for a few precious moments, they recaptured the joy of the friendship—everything felt just as it once had, untouched by time or illness.

What a powerful example of willpower expressed through perseverance.

The trainer never abandoned the friendship and never gave up. Instead, they reclaimed the closeness of that bond and replaced dis-ease with the ease of smiles and laughter.

The trainer chose to fight for the friendship—to honor and celebrate it, no matter the circumstances.

You might find yourself thinking how sad that situation is, or how strong you would need to be to handle it.

But don't miss the message by overlooking two simple yet powerful elements: opportunity and response.

The trainer's opportunity and response reveal the two essential ingredients for becoming the best version of yourself.

When you know who you are, and think without limitation about what you can do, anything becomes possible.

You have that same power, that same ability to make the most of even the hardest circumstances.

Here's how:

You have to really want to.

When your desire for a solution exceeds the limits of comfort, acceptance, or compromise, you're on the path to something extraordinary.

But you have to believe.

As Descartes said, "I think, therefore I am."

You are who you think you are.

That single truth determines whether you rise or fall, succeed or surrender.

You have to be selfless.

Your response to any experience, good or bad, is your personal signature.

When you show up wholeheartedly, with courage and sincerity, you create a mark that endures.

So ask yourself: How are you signing off on the situations in your life?

Know that you can, and know that you will—and you'll never suffer the perils of an ego clouded by doubt or confusion.

You have the power.

Now it's simply a matter of making it your will.

DAILY AFFIRMATIONS:

"I can do anything I set my mind to and endure anything that I ask my heart to."

"When I am selfless, the definition of who and what I am rests in the experience itself."

"Love's truest light is in its expression thereof."

"It's Your World"

"It takes as much energy to wish as it does to plan." —*Eleanor Roosevelt*

Organization starts in your mind and works its way outward. It shapes how you think, how you speak, and how you show up in the world.

When your thoughts are scattered and your mind is filled with unfinished business, it's hard to communicate clearly or express how you really feel.

You can't think straight when there's mental clutter taking up space.

When you're feeling unsettled, it's even harder to make the kind of lifestyle changes that strengthen your mind, body, and soul.

Gaining control, real control, over your life starts with your mindset, your surroundings, and your preparation.

That's where order comes in.

Simple word, big meaning.

Let's be honest, it's something almost everyone struggles with on a daily basis.

Because so much of what you want, like peace, progress, and clarity, often gets buried under distraction.

Scattered thoughts, personal issues, health concerns, relationship challenges, financial pressures . . . all of it can cloud your mind and slow your momentum.

But here's the truth: you can change that because order is attainable.

It's not impossible.

It's doable.

When you get your mind, body, and soul—what I like to call your Healthy House—in order, everything else starts to align.

Examine "Your World"

Let's talk about your world—the one you live in every single day.

It's both your inner space and the physical environment that surrounds you.

Your world speaks volumes about you.

The state of your home, your workspace, even your car—all of it paints a picture of who you are and how you're managing your life.

It reflects your ability to handle stress, organize time, and maintain emotional balance.

So take a look around.

What does your space say about you right now?

Organize and thrive.

Evaluate "Your World"

Now, don't just look—search for meaning.

Because when you look with intention, answers often appear.

Ask yourself what truly serves you. What brings you peace, strength, and progress?

Be honest about what doesn't.

How about the people, habits, and situations that no longer serve your greater good?

It's time to reevaluate and prioritize.

Don't let obstacles turn into permanent roadblocks. Break down those walls, and let what really matters rise to the top.

Put your faith where it belongs.

Trust those who've earned it.

Hold yourself accountable, embrace change, and give yourself permission to start fresh.

Organize and thrive.

Manage "Your World"

Now here's something I want you to really take in:

You have to take charge to be in charge.

Say it again with me—you have to take charge to be in charge.

Being in charge of your life means paying attention to what's coming in and what's going out—your thoughts, your energy, your habits, your relationships.

Take charge and choose to care.

Believe in your worth.

Take charge and eat to nourish your body.

Take charge and move daily so your body can support your goals.

Take charge and strengthen your faith so that all your relationships, including the one with yourself, stay aligned and whole.

You already have the time, the energy, and the ability to organize and thrive.

Remember, order doesn't mean perfection, it simply means positioning yourself for success.

When you organize your mind, body, and soul, you create a foundation strong enough to support real, lasting change—in your world.

DAILY AFFIRMATIONS:

*"I am creating balance and order in my life,
one intentional choice at a time."*

*"I trust myself to make decisions that honor my
peace, my purpose, and my potential."*

"I am showing up for myself today—with clarity, courage, and compassion."

REFLECTION
"I Got Your Six"

Six o'clock is straight behind you and sets up the best strike zone. WWI pilots were the first to say, "I got your six," meaning they've got you covered, so the enemy can't come up behind your back and kill you. "I got your six" means "I got your back."

Some of the most valued people in life are the ones who have your back, the ones you know you can always count on.

While few truly fit that description, everyone needs at least one person who stands firmly in their corner.

Because loyalty is trust.

It's dependability.

It's the quiet assurance that you are not alone.

At its best, loyalty is both given and received. It's a bond built on respect, honesty, and genuine care.

If you've ever wondered what loyalty really looks like, here are a few unmistakable signs:

Loyal people celebrate each other's success as though it were their own.

They are genuine and honest in their opinions and motives.

They prioritize each other's well-being.

They respect and honor boundaries.

They cherish the relationship and work tirelessly to preserve it.

Loyalty is rare and precious. When it's needed, it often must rise to the occasion without hesitation—sometimes at a moment's notice.

No more, no less, loyalty is one of the purest demonstrations of honor.

Stay loyal to your beliefs, your values, yourself, and to those who truly matter in your life.

Because loyalty is more than a choice; it's a responsibility—a commitment that strengthens every bond it touches.

It is the foundation for lasting success: in relationships, in teamwork, in leadership, and in your own personal growth.

Whether in friendship, marriage, sports, work, or self-care, the power of loyalty remains the same, it unites, it uplifts, and it endures.

DAILY AFFIRMATIONS:

"I remain loyal to my values, even when life challenges my strength."

"I show up each day with honesty, consistency, and compassion in all my relationships."

"I choose to be someone others can count on.

"Exactly Where You Need to Be"

"The two most powerful warriors are patience and time." —Leo Tolstoy

Offering to be available for someone during their time of greatest need is one of the most powerful gestures you can make.

It can also be a substantial undertaking.

This kind of support requires clear boundaries, thoughtful intervention, and timely reserve. The ebb and flow of these requirements demands flexibility and resilience.

Every person is different.

Each has their own troubles, insecurities, predicaments, and ups and downs. Understanding this is essential when you choose to offer your support.

To truly support someone in their time of need means being present in the way that person needs, whether that's by phone, in person, or even from afar. You don't have to be prepared; you simply have to be willing and understanding.

Sometimes, "being there" doesn't require physical presence or even a single word. That kind of silent support can be incredibly powerful.

There is no greater security than knowing someone is there for you, regardless of how long it's been since you last spoke.

To be that kind of friend or partner is a priceless gift.

At the same time, be prepared to go with the flow.

Your own priorities might need to be set aside for a while as the person you're supporting works through what they need. If you find yourself wanting to do more than is necessary, recognize that sometimes more than what is needed is just more.

Be there when it's time, but only as long as you're needed. Let patience and time guide the extent of your involvement.

Remember, giving love and support in the way it's truly needed, rather than in the way you feel it should be given, is the difference between helping someone else versus helping yourself feel needed.

Consider creating a personal creed of supportive intention—a simple statement you can refer to as a reminder of how to offer your support wisely.

Here's an example you can use or adapt:

"I will not give, only offer ... I will not advise, only show ... I will not control, only support ... I am not the path; I am the light that illuminates the path."

The goal of lending help and support is to act with selfless love, understanding, and presence—giving what is needed without attachment to the outcome.

DAILY AFFIRMATIONS:

"When I feel unappreciated or left out, I know I am still within the heart and soul of those I support."

"I am strong enough and secure enough to understand that silence doesn't mean I've been forgotten."

"I don't need to be the first to come to mind, nor do I need to be summoned at all, to understand that my existence is equally as strong as my physical presence."

CHAPTER 6

Sharpen Your Vision

*Clarity isn't about seeing more—it's about
seeing what truly matters.*

Welcome to the final section of the book.

Here you will find a connection with reflections designed to guide you
through self-reflection, nurture your self-awareness, and gently explore
your daily actions and thought processes.

This experience begins with the quiet spark of self-discovery and gently
unfolds into building meaningful relationships, overcoming challenges,
growing personally, and communicating effectively—all while aligning
with the natural rhythm of your life.

Each part flows naturally into the next, creating a cohesive guide that
not only broadens your outlook but also empowers you to embrace every
moment with clarity and purpose.

As you read these pages, you'll discover practical, down-to-earth guidance
that helps harmonize your inner world with your everyday experiences,

fostering a deeper, more compassionate connection with yourself and the world around you.

These reflections are about:

- Self-Reflection
- Self-Awareness
- Daily actions, thought processes

Foundations of Self-Awareness & Personal Identity

"Self-Identity"

*"Yesterday I was clever, so I wanted to change the world.
Today I am wise, so I am changing myself." —Rumi*

When you were a kid, the big question was always: "What do you want to be when you grow up?"

Years later, that same question often transforms into something else—a wish to reconnect with your younger self.

Maybe you wish you still had the energy and health of your youth, no silver hairline, fewer wrinkles, or even just the chance to do a few things differently—to make better choices knowing what you know now.

It's natural to think this way; who hasn't had those moments of reflection?

Yet some people never quite figure out what they truly want to be, or even what they want out of life.

At the heart of it all lies one essential truth: the key to fulfillment is understanding your self-identity. While that identity naturally evolves with time, nothing compares to truly knowing yourself on a deeper level.

So, how do you figure out who you are, what your true identity really is?

That question can be one of life's greatest challenges.

Let's start by doing a simple check-in—a personal "ID check."

Check Your ID

Are you still working and hoping for a promotion, or are you considering a career change?

Are you thinking about retirement, and if so, what does that look like for you?

Has your role shifted to include caring for a parent or loved one?

Have your family dynamics changed?

Are you now an empty nester?

Is your child married?

Are your kids having kids, making you a proud grandparent?

Are you single and navigating what's next?

Has your health changed in ways that require new habits or lifestyle adjustments?

Has your relationship status changed—newly married, remarried, or widowed?

This is only a short list of the life transitions that reshape not just what you do, but who you are, to yourself and to others.

As if that weren't enough, the question of identity remains in constant motion as you age.

That's why exercises like this "ID check" are both invaluable and necessary from time to time.

Your Private Changing Room

You're constantly changing because life is always changing.

Your body feels it.

Your heart knows it.

But sometimes your mind takes longer to catch up.

When that happens, we can lose sight of who we've become.

Think of this process as stepping into your Private Changing Room—a sacred space you create for privacy and reflection. It's not about clothes or appearances, but about giving yourself room to pause, ponder, and notice which roles and identities still fit, and which ones you may have outgrown.

The mirror in your Private Changing Room doesn't just reflect your face. It reflects your evolution, the ongoing story of who you are becoming.

Use these TrAction Steps to Stay Current with Yourself:

At Home: Look in the mirror and describe who you are with family or friends.

Outside of Home: Look in the mirror again and describe who you are in your work or community roles.

Your Authentic Self: Finally, describe to yourself who you are at your core — including the qualities few people, or no one, may know about.

Final Reflection

Self-reflection is a powerful tool, the mark of a wisdom seeker.

Discovering who you are, who you want to be, and who you are capable of becoming is always within your reach.

Start now.

Look within, and become the best possible version of yourself—one that changes with time, not against it.

DAILY AFFIRMATIONS:

"When I need support, I promise to be my own best friend."

"Change is not my enemy; it's my evolution."

"I give myself permission to outgrow versions of me that no longer fit."

"The Truth of Understanding"

*"Any fool can know. The point is to
understand." —Albert Einstein*

By that which we give, we also receive.

Do you truly understand the choices you're making and why?

Do you recognize the reasons behind the way you feel, the good and the not so good, and how they shape your experiences?

Do you feel understood—by your spouse, your friends, your family, your coworkers, and most importantly, by yourself?

A little understanding goes a long way.

Whether silent or spoken, granted or received, understanding is the fertile ground from which peace, love, and happiness grow.

So, what does it take to practice understanding?

Show interest.

You are already halfway there when you are eager and open to listen and learn. Listen with compassion, and you will begin to understand while being understood yourself.

Be patient.

The deepest understanding unfolds over time—moment by moment, experience by experience. This is how relationships take root and thrive.

When understanding fades, relationships falter.

Remain open-minded.

Resist the urge to pre-judge or draw conclusions without all the facts. Those are the seeds of misunderstanding that often grow into regret.

Consciously listen.

Listen with the intent to learn something new.

Open both your heart and your mind, giving your full attention. The difference between simply hearing and truly understanding is when words begin to resonate as thoughts, feelings, and emotions.

What Does It Take to Feel Understood?

It begins with understanding yourself.

Take time to reflect on what you want, what you need, what you are feeling—and why. Those discoveries create the path for others to follow when learning to understand you.

Communicate your feelings.

Express what's in your heart in a way that truly conveys how you feel.

Own it.

The better you know yourself, the easier it becomes to share yourself with others.

Build trust.

You must first trust yourself before you can trust someone else to understand you.

View trust as strength—not as a risk.

Allow it.

Let others in.

Allow them the chance to understand you.

That requires vulnerability, and with it comes the courage to be seen and heard for who you really are.One of the most powerful lessons in life is realizing that understanding, and being understood, requires active participation.

Both are born from self-awareness, patience, and the willingness to give as openly as you wish to receive.

So go forward and, in the name of understanding, give effortlessly and receive graciously.

DAILY AFFIRMATIONS:

"I know I am evolving because I am still learning new things about myself."

"I will fight through false feelings of insecurity by giving myself permission to seek and understand what I really need."

"I am giving myself the support and understanding I need to thrive and succeed."

REFLECTION

"Like Me"

*"The privilege of a lifetime is to become
who you really are." —Carl Jung*

The most important and influential relationship you will ever have is the one you have with yourself.

Recognizing that truth is the first step toward truly understanding and appreciating who you are. It is the foundational blueprint for success, happiness, love, and self-fulfillment.

Brené Brown said it best: *"Owning our story and loving ourselves through that process is the bravest thing we'll ever do."*

It's that process—the commitment and follow-through, that brings you closer to your true self, creating inner peace, confidence, and a lasting sense of well-being.

Remember, it is far wiser to seek to understand yourself than to be understood by others, for it only takes the shallow opinion of one fool to disturb the calm of an unsettled mind.

So who likes you?

Who sees you?

Who loves you?

First and foremost, it must be you.

You must be the example of what you value by believing in yourself.

You must see yourself as you wish to be seen by shaping the signature of your persona.

You must love yourself before you can fully receive love in return.

These truths form the foundation of self-acceptance and authentic living.

But like anything truly worthwhile, it takes work—and practice.

Start now.

It's time to love yourself, respect yourself, forgive yourself, and nurture yourself.

Begin with these daily steps:

Be yourself.

The best you can ever be is who you truly are.

"Care about what other people think and you will always be their prisoner."
—Lao Tzu

Embrace yourself.

Self-acceptance is the key to lasting strength.

"To be yourself in a world that is constantly trying to make you something else is the greatest accomplishment." —Ralph Waldo Emerson

Reinvent yourself—again and again.

You are always just one decision away from becoming the best version of yourself.

"When I let go of what I am, I become what I might be." —Lao Tzu

DAILY AFFIRMATIONS:

"I trust my journey and embrace the person I am becoming."

"I choose to love, respect, and forgive myself—daily."

"I am my own source of confidence, peace, and strength."

Building Trust & Strengthening Relationships

"Trustworthy"

"Be true to your work, your word, and your friend." —Henry David Thoreau

What do we have—and who are we—without trust?

Not much.

Stephen Covey once said, *"Trust is the glue of life. It's the most essential ingredient in effective communication. It's the foundational principle that holds all relationships."*

Trust sits at the very center of your existence, and from it, all good or bad things flow. Nothing replaces it, and few things hurt more than when it's broken.

Whether you're working to earn someone's trust or deciding whether to give it, remember this: trust doesn't always come easily. The decision to trust—or not—requires awareness, wisdom, and discernment.

Trust Is Born Within

How to trust is instinctive.

When to trust is learned.

Why you trust is what gives meaning to the decision itself.

This is why you must discover your own best way to arrive at the answer that satisfies the question:

Why should I trust?

Here's a great way to get started: The "Trust" Quiz

Take a moment and explore your personal relationship with trust. Your answers will reveal a lot about how you view yourself, others, and the world around you.

1. *What is your definition of trust?*
2. *Don't look it up—write the first words that come to mind.*
3. *Do you trust yourself?*
4. *Be raw and honest, and write a detailed explanation of why or why not.*
5. *Who trusts you the most?*
6. *List only those you know trust you, and explain why they do.*
7. *What does it take to earn your trust?*
8. *Be specific and describe the qualities or actions that build trust for you.*
9. *What is your philosophy on trust?*
10. *Write about how you feel, how important it is, and what role it plays in all areas of your life.*
11. *Answering these questions sharpens your vision—your insight, your hindsight, and your foresight.*

Now that you've explored your personal foundation of trust, it's time to evaluate how you extend that trust to others.

How you trust begins with what you believe.

What constitutes trust, when it should be given, how it is earned, and whether it can be repaired are all reflections of those beliefs.

Whether you are striving to build new trust or repair broken trust, the process is the same, because what strengthens is also capable of repair.

Below are the 5 building blocks of trust that can help strengthen or repair the bonds of marriage and family dynamics, improve the quality of your friendships, and increase your overall sense of peace and well-being.

The Five Building Blocks of Trust

Transparency

Be open and honest. When you do, you shift the decision to trust away from yourself and onto others. Being your authentic self is always enough—and for the right people, it's everything.

Dependability

Offer the same quality, energy, and intention day after day. When people know where you stand, they immediately know where they stand too.

Consistency

More powerful than how something begins or ends is the commitment to show up, again and again, without fail. Consistency creates structure, builds respect, and quietly communicates love, safety, and security.

Reliability

There is no greater honor than being someone's "go-to." Your true character shines when you answer the call and fill a need. You don't have to force the right timing, the universe knows your heart and will place you exactly where you are needed.

Accountability

Own your actions, both the missteps and the milestones. Growth is a process, not perfection. There is no room for judgment when progress is being made, and you are a work in progress.

Remember

Trust is personal; you must first trust yourself.

Trust is part of love; you can't truly love without it.

Trust is a measure of strength, put in the work and the return will be your reward.

Trust is essential; it is the main ingredient in the success of all relationships.

Trust in the process and prosper.

DAILY AFFIRMATIONS:

"I trust my ability to handle anything that comes my way."

"I am grateful for the relationships I have in my life and the trust I share within those relationships."

"I trust in the power of positive thinking."

"The Five Relationship Agreements"

"Do what you did in the beginning of a relationship and there won't be an end." —Tony Robbins

There is a sweet spot in relationships.

But it can be tricky to find.

It's that balance between expectations and boundaries.

Relationships in and of themselves are mutual agreements between two people that take shape in the form of friendships, marriages, and family connections.

Like any agreement or contract of sorts, there are terms of engagement and boundaries that are represented by each person's thoughts, feelings, beliefs, needs, and past experiences.

It is the recipe for harmony when all is well or for discord when there is a violation or breakdown of one or more of the five basic relationship agreements.

The Five Relationship Agreements:

Agree to Trust: Trust is delicate and must be practiced repeatedly. Whether it is hard-earned or freely given, it must always be carefully preserved.

Agree to Honesty: Distinguish your needs from your desires, and be truthful with yourself and others about them. Clear honesty strengthens understanding and connection.

Agree to Communication: When silence replaces words, intentions are often misunderstood. Whether you feel love or fear, sadness or joy, share your feelings openly.

Agree to Respect: You can agree to disagree, and at times you may feel hurt or angry. This is when it's important to remember the value you hold for each other. Whatever you decide, whatever you do—do it in the best interest of the relationship.

Agree to Appreciation: Nurture your relationships, including the one with yourself—through acknowledgment, support, praise, and humility are all opportunities to show appreciation. Take nothing for granted and let your appreciation show.

When practiced with commitment and genuine intention, these five agreements help manage conflict, reduce drama, and ease needless emotional suffering. They infuse happiness, personal freedom, love, and respect into every relationship.

In summary, practicing these agreements means trusting honestly, communicating openly and respectfully, and expressing humble appreciation for yourself and others.

When any one of these practices becomes difficult, it's time to revisit and maybe even renegotiate the terms of your sacred contract with the other person.

Don't wait.

Now is the time to renew the relationships that are the most important to you.

DAILY AFFIRMATIONS:

*"I'm going to show up for me—because the relationship I
have with myself deserves the same time and attention
that I would give to someone I care about."*

"I will take nothing for granted by practicing meaningful acts consistently."

"I have unconditional love for myself and those who truly care about me."

"The Art of Repair"

"The size of your success is measured by the strength of your desire; the size of your dream; and how you handle disappointment along the way." —Robert Kiyosaki

Disappointment is the seed from which regret grows, and if left unchecked, disappointment can lead to negativity.

Regret, sadness, anger, and even depression can arise when you feel as though you have been let down.

Sometimes it's hard to turn lemons into lemonade.

Truth is, disappointment comes in many forms and it affects everyone differently. Residual feelings of rejection, defeat, misunderstanding, and low self-esteem are among the most common outcomes.

How you manage your feelings and cope with disappointment is the key to recovery.

Jim Rohn said it best: "You must learn to discipline your disappointment."

Whether it's mustering up the strength to forgive or to open your heart and trust again, it takes a certain discipline.

You have to trust yourself.

No one knows you better than you. Check in with yourself—ask what you need, listen to what you're thinking and feeling, and trust your instincts. That is the true art of intuition.

You must gain perspective.

There's always another side—another possibility waiting to be seen. When you examine every point of view with equal openness, you gain the power of perspective.

You have to communicate.

It isn't enough to simply feel your emotions: that's just the starting point. To help process what you're feeling, you must express it—speak your thoughts, share your truth. There can be no flow if you don't let go.

You must use patience.

Healing takes time when it's real. Patience is the soil from which new chances grow. Give yourself time to heal, and give others a chance to reflect, rebound, and repair. Remember, time is a proven healer.

You have to embrace inner change.

Seek opportunities to create joy and success in new ways. When you change your mind, you change your life.

Don't let disappointment define your day or your outlook on the future. Disappointments are not failures—they're answers revealed while you're still learning how to make things better.

Finding balance between your successes and setbacks is how you minimize future disappointments and grow stronger with every experience.

Remember, every disappointment gives you the opportunity to make another appointment with success.

DAILY AFFIRMATIONS:

"Disappointments are pauses, not the endings."

"Chance is the key that unlocks change—and I'm taking it."

"Challenges may test my desire—but I got this!"

Embracing Faith &
Overcoming Obstacles

"Push Beyond Belief"

"To one who has faith, no explanation is necessary. To one without faith, no explanation is possible." —*Thomas Aquinas*

Time to bounce back?

Sometimes it's not so easy. Let's face it—there are moments when you feel hurt, defeated, and less than your true value.

When those experiences come along, it's only natural to wonder why things are going the way they are. Finding meaning in the midst of pain can feel confusing and, at times, impossible.

Whether you are feeling spiritually, mentally, or physically weak, there's definitely a way to bounce back.

Since shaking it off or trying to ignore what's going on seldom works, you have to find the courage to face what is really going on. You don't have to be strong to do this—in fact, you probably won't be—but you do have to be willing.

You have to have FAITH.

Faith is one of life's greatest strengths and most vital resources. But it's not something you can fake or force—so maybe that's why so many people struggle to find it.

Having faith means believing in something or someone (especially yourself) even when there is no visible sign or logical reason to believe.

Trusting without seeing *is* the true practice of having faith.

Imagine how differently your hardest moments might feel if you chose faith instead of fear. You would still face challenges, but would manage them with greater peace, less stress and more confidence in what the outcome could be.

Sounds good, but how can you do that?

Building faith takes practice and consistency.

Start by grounding yourself.

Surrender the urge to control every detail of a difficult situation. Do what you can, then allow life to naturally unfold—with patience, trust, and faith that things will work themselves out in time.

I adopted this passage written by Jackson Kiddard as my personal **"Faith Instead of Fear Creed"**:

Anything that annoys you is teaching you patience.

Anyone who abandons you is teaching you how to stand up on your own two feet.

Anything that angers you is teaching you forgiveness and compassion.

Anything that has power over you is teaching you how to take your power back.

Anything you hate is teaching you unconditional love.

Anything you fear is teaching you courage to overcome your fear.

Anything you can't control is teaching you how to let go.

I read this every day because you become what you think about, and without regular attention, faith can be fleeting.

Push beyond your belief and have a little faith.

Everything is going to be okay!

DAILY AFFIRMATIONS:

"I trust because trust is the practice of faith—the greatest personal resource of all. I am worthy of that faith within myself, and by giving it freely, I remain ready, willing, and open to receive it in return."

"I am free because the true power of faith is its endless, boundless potential to create and conceive whatever the heart can feel and the mind can see."

"I am strong because I choose faith over fear. In that choice, I see truth, direction, and purpose. I remain humble in my faith, knowing it is not a possession but a decision—one I choose to make every day."

"What's in Your Way"

*Obstacles" do not block the path, they
are the path." —Zen Proverb*

Sometimes words just get in the way.

Most of the time, you get in your own way.

Excuses, sabotaging choices, limiting beliefs—they all contribute to creating the obstacles that you feel are blocking you from reaching your end goal.

If you change your thoughts, you can change your mind—and that shift gives you the power, motivation, and courage to go after what you want.

That's a pretty powerful statement.

It's not easy but it's true, and with the right tools and practice, it is indeed something that you can do.

Here's a great example:

A high school track athlete came to me for coaching. She was fast and consistently posted great times but never won any of her races.

She remarked at how weak she was and felt as though previous injuries were also holding her back from running her fastest and winning.

She told her coach she thought old injuries were holding her back, and that she planned to start physical therapy.

I asked her to run so I could observe. She ran fast and looked strong.

Afterward, she smiled widely and said, "I could run even faster, but you didn't ask me to run my fastest."

Then she asked, "What's wrong with me? Why can't I run like that at my meets?"

It wasn't her strength or speed holding her back—it was fear. She feared success and was subconsciously sabotaging herself by slowing down, pulling up, and thinking herself right out of the race.

This challenge is far more common than most realize. It often feels safer to *want* success from a place of supposed disadvantage than to actually pursue and achieve it.

Fear of success is a subtle, self-imposed obstacle fueled by self-doubt. It limits, frustrates, and controls, often without being recognized for what it truly is.

Try these TrAction Steps to help work through the fear of success:

Identify what you believe is standing between you and your goals.

Check in with yourself: does the idea of success fill you with excitement, or with apprehension?

Reframe limiting beliefs by replacing fear-based impossibilities with empowering possibilities. In other words, change your thought process.

Remember, your success starts from within!

DAILY AFFIRMATIONS:

"I release fear and embrace my full potential with confidence and courage."

"I am capable of achieving what I desire, and I move forward without hesitation."

"Every challenge I face strengthens my determination and fuels my success."

Personal Growth Through Actions & Mindset

"Don't Miss Your Take"

"Good judgment comes from experience, and experience comes from bad judgment." —Rita Mae Brown

How would you know if you were coming or going, getting closer or further away, or understanding right from wrong if you didn't make any mistakes in life?

Yet perfection seems to be the goal when it's really an illusion. It is the art of attainment, the act of practice, the persistence of patience that brings us what we really want, the one thing that we need to see to journey on, and that is progress.

Don't miss your takeaway.

Don't make the mistake of thinking or feeling as though you can't make a mistake. Your greatest opportunities to grow happen when you don't get it right.

It's one of the most organic forms of learning.

Mistakes are the changes and unexpected lessons learned that guide you and turn you about-face so that you can start down the path of healing and redemption.

Whether it is personal or professional, mistakes often answer some of the most common questions. Where do you go from here, what should you do next, what is best for you now and for the future?

When you recover from mistakes, it is important to pursue the solution with the humility of a spirit that seeks healing.

There's a difference between learning and simply making up your mind to avoid anything having to do with the experience related to that mistake. Face it and learn from it; otherwise, you will see the same error in your ways over and over again.

You will make mistakes; they are a part of life. But the question is:

Are you getting the most out of your mistakes?

Here is a list of steps to take after you've made a mistake:

Accept the mistake and humbly acknowledge it (own it)

Reflect upon what happened (how, why, etc.) (learn from it)

Render repair for your mistake (if possible) and sincerely apologize for it (atonement)

Apologize in person if at all possible (sincerity)

Offer a healthy solution if possible (take action)

Do your part and allow the situation or other person to do theirs by allowing time and space (patience)

Understanding is powerful; employ empathy in the words you speak (genuineness)

Be kind to yourself (compassion)

Learn from your mistake (reflect and grow)

Forgiveness from another is a gift; forgiving yourself is a blessing.

Remember...

You are human.

You are not perfect.

You will make mistakes.

You will stumble at times.

You will fall and get hurt.

BUT

You are needed.

You are enough.

You are growing.

You will rise and soar.

You will be just fine.

Don't miss your take-away, your chance to grow to become a better version of the person you were even just a moment ago.

DAILY AFFIRMATIONS:

"I am not perfect, I am progress."

"Every mistake is a chance to grow."

"Effort is the rain that blooms mistakes into improvement, therefore, I never stop trying."

"You Have the Strength"

"Everything you need is within you, the strength, courage and confidence to change your life. You just need to look inside yourself and find it." —Amanda Ray

Strength ...

It is one of the most sought after, admired, and talked-about qualities a person can possess.

You and everyone you know has some measure of strength within. Strength comes in many forms, expressed as character traits, talents, skills or personal attributes.

Drawing upon your strengths begins with understanding what they are.

If you're not yet fully aware of your strengths, give yourself the gift of discovering them.

Figuring out your strengths—what you know, what comes naturally, and what you've worked hard to develop, is the first step toward using them with intention and confidence.

Employers, friends, and relationship partners alike are naturally interested in your strengths. They reveal what you can contribute, what you bring to the table, and the value you offer.

Take a few minutes right now and think about what your strengths might be.

Remember, there's no shame in acknowledging the strengths you don't have. The honor comes from recognizing and using the strengths you do have to their fullest potential.

How to find your strengths:

Examine your personality.

Explore your talents.

Review your accomplishments.

Consider your interests.

Evaluate your natural abilities.

Listen to compliments.

Pay attention to what motivates you.

Finding honest positives within each of these strength-finding areas helps you hold yourself accountable to a fair standard that benefits both you and everyone around you.

Playing to your strengths means trusting yourself and believing in the best you have to offer.

When in doubt or in fear, stop and repeat this mantra as many times as necessary:

I AM, I CAN, and I WILL because . . .

I am WISE.

I am WORTHY.

I am FEARLESS.

I am STRONG.

I am ENOUGH.

Speak your truth into existence.

Claim and declare your strength today and every day, because it's far better to believe you are strong—even stronger than you realize—when it comes to taking full advantage of the power of your mind.

When your will aligns with your power, you gain the confidence to move forward, the strength to endure, and the patience to sustain and accomplish whatever you desire.

DAILY AFFIRMATIONS:

"I speak strength, confidence, and courage into my life—my words shape my reality."

"My greatest strengths are my strongest beliefs."

"Healing and recovery are strengths, which means I've been strong all of my life"

REFLECTION

"Just a Minute"

"Optimism isn't believing nothing bad will happen. It's about believing in your ability to handle it when it does." —Mel Robbins

There's a Bob Marley song that reminds us:

"Every little thing is going to be alright."

Too often, we become so consumed with looking ahead—anticipating "what's next"—that we overlook the small, amazing moments that are happening all around us.

Moments like someone stopping and allowing you to merge in traffic.

Or the simple fact that your body allows you to walk, talk, and breathe with ease.

These moments are the little things that make up life—each one a quiet reminder that everything *little* thing really is alright.

Life may not be perfect or exactly as you envisioned it, but more often than not, there are far more things going right than wrong.

A quick gratitude check reminds us that we have so very much to be grateful for.

When distractions pile up and emotional fatigue clouds your focus, remember—you can redirect your energy. You can choose to see what's good and manage stress with perspective and appreciation.

It's up to you to illuminate the bright side.

There is a Tibetan saying that reminds us, *"If you take care of the minutes, the years take care of themselves."*

So, work with what you've got, be the best to who you're with, accept what you cannot change, and, like water, make the obstacles that impede your path a part of the path itself continuing on as though uninterrupted.

DAILY AFFIRMATIONS:

"I choose to focus on what is going right and let gratitude guide my perspective

"I choose humility because it is the seed from which gratefulness grows."

"I am going to look on the bright side and consider the positive in every negative experience."

Effective Communication & Legacy

"What's in a Word"

"If we understood the power of our thoughts, we would guard them more closely. If we understood the awesome power of our words, we would prefer silence to almost anything negative. In our thoughts and words, we create our own weaknesses and our own strengths. Our limitations and joys begin in our hearts. We can always replace negative with positive." —Betty Eadie

I've heard it said that sometimes words just get in the way. I like to think, however, that words actually pave the way to better understanding and clear communication.

Words shape your thoughts and feelings, your actions and reactions, and virtually every decision you make.

Finding the right words can be difficult, and even harder to express, especially when you're feeling anxious.

The best thing to do is to slow down. Take the time and space you need to think, breathe, and process what has been said. Acknowledge what you're feeling, then speak with purpose and understanding.

It isn't easy, but this is the wisdom of thinking before you speak. This minimizes the chances of saying something that you might regret later.

It's worth it, because words can make or break a relationship, and your choice of words and the way you express yourself can make or break your marriage, your career, your friendships, and even your own self-esteem.

Practice the art of slowing down and infusing mindfulness into your day by increasing self-awareness through the power of humble recognition.

Read the following declarations. They are very powerful reminders, and when acknowledged with a humble conscience, they become the guiding light for living with intention and contentment:

Six Mindfulness Reminders

Words are powerful.

"Words have energy and power with the ability to help, to heal, to hinder, to hurt, to harm, to humiliate, and to humble." —Yehuda Berg

Words are useful.

"Raise your words, not your voice. It is rain that grows flowers, not thunder." —Rumi

Words are history.

"Be careful with your words. Once they are said, they can only be forgiven, not forgotten." —Unknown

Words are necessary.

"Don't ever diminish the power of words. Words move hearts and hearts move limbs." —Hamza Yusuf

Words are meaningful.

"Be mindful when it comes to your words. A string of some that don't mean much to you may stick with someone else for a lifetime." —Rachel Wolchin

Words are forever.

"Words are seeds that do more than blow around. They land in our hearts and not the ground. Be careful what you plant and careful what you say. You might have to eat what you planted one day." —Unknown

Words are the touches that leave imprints on the souls of those who hear them. Remember, you can build, break, mend, or destroy a relationship in just a few words.

DAILY AFFIRMATIONS:

"I understand that when I mean what I say, explaining is easy to do."

"I am going to speak with intention, using words that heal, uplift, and inspire."

"Mere words are just that until shaped by how, when, where, and why they were spoken."

"Your Message Matters"

*"My legacy is that I stayed on course ... from
the beginning to the end, because I believed in
something inside of me."* —Tina Turner

Not to be confused with hopes or dreams, there is a legacy that exists within each and every one of us.

Who you are, what you have done, and what you mean to others are all essential pieces of what a legacy is made of.

It does not require fame, fortune, or a spotlight. Legacy is about the essence of you—the unspoken message that continues to echo long after you've moved on.

The effect of your personality, your kindness, your friendship, and all the wonderful qualities that make you unique—those are what give a memorable legacy its power.

Your legacy is your message.

It is your personal imprint on the lives of others and the world around you. It is powerful enough to shape someone's life without you even realizing it.

So what's your legacy going to be?

Consider this as you reflect and craft your own:

Understand who you are. Take into consideration your opinions, talents, likes and dislikes, beliefs, personal goals, and accomplishments. Then summarize your thoughts into five words or less to describe yourself.

Identify your passion. Describe at least one thing in life that deeply resonates with you—a topic, hobby, talent, occupation, person, or cause. It doesn't have to be something you did before. Choose what captivates you.

Share your message. Think of your legacy as a treasure chest that holds the words and values that define you, including one thing in life that really resonates with you the most. Write an impact statement—a short, heartfelt summary that captures your purpose and what you stand for.

Whether or not you believe it to be true, your mere existence makes a meaningful impact. Chances are, you have no idea of just how profound that impact is, but it is.

Don't underestimate it.

Embrace it and spend each day crafting, refining, and living the legacy of your message.

DAILY AFFIRMATIONS:

*"My presence in the lives of others makes a difference.
How amazing that will be is up to me."*

"I will brushstroke the story of my legacy against the canvas of my life with shades of heartfelt intentions and positive attitudes."

"I am proud of what I stand for."

"Message in a Bottle"

"A candle loses nothing by lighting another." —James Keller

There is a gift so powerful and amazing that it does not matter if you are the giver or the recipient.

The impact is that profound.

It's the pathway to freedom.

The recipe for HEALING.

And . . .

It truly is a gift that keeps on giving.

It is the gift of listening—without judgment, without opinion.

Just LISTENING.

Hard to find, indeed.

But absolutely necessary.

I once offered a friend the opportunity to tell me their story—their version, their feelings, while holding nothing back.

Whatever came to mind—secrets, guilty truths, dreams, fears, goals, regrets—was open for discussion.

The result was more than just a release of tears and emotions.

It was a chance to divide the weight of woe by two.

There's something profoundly healing about knowing that at least one person in the world sees you, hears you, and understands how you feel.

It's very freeing.

Everyone needs to be heard at some point and needs to feel understood—without judgment or conditions.

All too often people imprison themselves with suppressed feelings and emotions that dim the true spirit of their being.

This triggers stress, pain, illness, and negativity.

It weakens the power of positive thinking and limits your ability to fully embrace some of the most wonderful things in life like peace, love, and joy.

You need, and the world needs, the best version of you that you have to offer.

So, if something has been weighing on your heart, the best way to navigate your way through it is to let it out.

Find a trusted listener and share your story.

Don't keep it in, let it go.

Enjoy the freedom of *release*.

You deserve this!

DAILY AFFIRMATIONS:

"I honor my thoughts and feelings and seek to understand rather than dismiss them."

"I know how to be fully present, completely in the moment—all I have to do is listen."

"To listen is to give what everyone needs at one time or another . . . now I am listening to myself."

Embracing Life's Timing & Priorities

REFLECTION

"Trust the Timing of Your Life"

"We all have our time machines. Some take us back, they're called memories. Some take us forward, they're called dreams." —Jeremy Irons

Sometimes the best insurance is reassurance, and today I want you to know—everything is going to be okay.

How do I know that?

I know that you are exactly where you are meant to be, interacting with and impacting the lives of those you were intended to.

There is a greater plan, a bigger agenda, if you will, hard at work that is constantly moving and evolving.

Some call it fate; others describe it as destiny. Whatever you choose to believe, know this: your presence is required exactly where you are.

You're not stuck; you're simply not finished with the situation you're in, with the job you're at, or with the relationships you're in, otherwise you wouldn't be there.

Nothing happens by chance, though it may seem that way at times.

The people you meet, the ones you know, and even those you pass by without a word—-all of them are in the right place and time. Every encounter shapes both how you see yourself and how you influence others.

Each one is both a lesson, and a blessing.

The lessons you carry are meant for others—to remind, to inspire, and to awaken growth within them.

The lessons you receive are meant for you—to guide, to ground, and to help you evolve into your next, best version.

Through every interaction and experience, you are continuously growing. This is the beauty, and the challenge of self-evolution: the daily journey toward becoming a better friend, coworker, partner, parent, or person of faith.

Becoming the best possible version of your former self is a shared human goal.

You get the help you need every day to become the best possible version of yourself—through the opportunities, people, and moments that cross your path. Each one is divinely ordered. You just have to trust that you are exactly where you need to be.

Time is the heartbeat of patience.

Be still, not stagnant.

Listen for the silent whispers of guidance that surface when your mind is calm and open.

May these words find you, where you are, and remind you that you are already on the path meant for you.

Journey not with your feet—for it is the wind beneath that carries you.

DAILY AFFIRMATIONS:

"I will continue to practice patience with everyone and everything in my life."

*"I am exactly where I need to be—growing,
learning, and unfolding in divine time."*

*"I trust the process of my life; every encounter, challenge,
and blessing is shaping me for what's next."*

"It's Time"

"Life, if well lived, is long enough" —Seneca

As you age, you begin to appreciate the value of time. You cannot make up for lost or wasted time. But you can choose to spend the time that you have *wisely*.

In a typical year, you get

365 days . . .

8,760 hours . . .

525,600 minutes . . .

31,536,000 seconds . . .

What are you going to do with all that time?

Since no two days are exactly alike and there are no "do-overs,"—how, where, when, and with whom you will spend your time becomes very important.

The wise approach?

Prioritize your time.

As easy as that sounds, it can be overwhelming and for good reason. Our lives are busy and our days are often overscheduled.

Catchphrases like *"time management"* and *"work-life balance"* usually come up whenever time is discussed.

But honestly, how you choose to spend your time comes down to balance:

doing what must be done, while still leaving room for the things that make life meaningful.

To get the best of both worlds—spending time wisely and taking time to enjoy it, start by looking at your time demands.

To make it easy, create three lists.

Make a list of what *needs* to be done.

This list reveals your time commitments. To complete it, identify what absolutely must be done—often driven by fear of consequence, moral obligation, financial necessity, health, or relationships.

Make a list of what *should* be done.

This list captures your time essentials. It's about assigning value to what you know should be done and understanding why. You might include healthy habits, nurturing relationships, planning for the future, or managing life's transitions.

Make a list of what you would *like* to get done.

This list reflects your spare time—the things that bring joy, fulfillment, and personal satisfaction. Travel, hobbies, volunteer work, or even new goals all belong here.

Making the most of your time begins with *organizing* your time. You have to see the big picture to determine where your time has the most value.

When you spend your time in the right places, you find yourself with all the right faces—facing reality, facing the answers you seek, facing north.

There are no right or wrong answers, but when you look at your lists, ask yourself: How do I feel? What's missing? What needs to change?

Time is energy; you only get so much. How you spend it is often the difference between productivity and waste, happiness and discontent.

DAILY AFFIRMATIONS:

"I honor my time by spending it with intention and purpose."

"Time is the currency of life and I choose to spend it wisely."

*"I choose balance, allowing productivity and
peace to coexist within my day."*

"Enough Is Enough"

"All we have to decide is what to do with the time that is given us." —J.R.R. Tolkien

I have lived more than 20,609 days in my lifetime, including today. I have recorded memories, made friends, endured ups and downs, and shared in the celebrations of others' joy as well as my own.

The worth of a life well-lived is often measured in the total of experiences we capture and cherish in the memories we keep.

How you choose to live your life is the art of the pour.

The energy you devote to your work, the attention you invest in your relationships, and the love and care you pour into your own happiness are all part of what makes your life whole.

Have you lived a life worth living so far?

More important than the answer itself is the daily practice of asking that question.

Getting what you need is not only necessary, it is essential to your happiness.

Remember, there's something in this life for everyone. What you get out of it is entirely up to you.

Deep within your mind, body, and soul, you already know what you want—and what you need.

Consider the following questions when evaluating the life you have lived so far:

Do you have any major regrets that weigh heavily on your heart?

If you do, now is the time to release them. Let go, and move forward instead of sitting still in negativity.

What accomplishments are you most proud of?

The size of those accomplishments matters little; what truly counts is how they make you feel. Celebrate your life with passion and appreciation.

What makes you the happiest?

Whether it's a person, a special place, or something that brings you peace, what matters most is how it makes you feel. Connect with those positive sources of energy every day.

It's your life; it's your story to write.

You are the author, and only you can decide when the time comes if you have lived a fulfilled life.

Because if *you* say it so, then enough is enough.

DAILY AFFIRMATIONS:

"I choose happiness, abundance and peace in my life."

"I release the weight of regret and carry forward only the wisdom and strength I've gained along the way."

"I'm giving my all, so there's nothing left to regret."

Nurturing Growth & Continuous Improvement

REFLECTION

"Nurture Your Blessings"

"A dream doesn't die because it has no truth. It dies because you fail to nurture it." —Susie Clevenger

It's easy to take what you already have for granted.

Whether it is good health, a meaningful relationship with a friend or significant other, sufficient income or any of your other daily necessities, we often seem to appreciate these things less as time goes on.

How many times have you thought—or said—what you wish you had done after the moment has passed?

It doesn't have to be that way and, surprisingly, there is no secret time-management hack.

The solution is simple.

Be fully present whenever you arrive, wherever you are, and for however long you have the chance to be in the moment.

Take nothing for granted and you will be rewarded with the wonderful experience of genuine appreciation in place of regret.

Nurture your health, your mind, your spiritual beliefs, your time, your relationships and your connections with people, places, pets, and whatever else is of great importance to you.

Don't just nurture what you love, nurture what you need.

Start right NOW.

Nurturing may look different for you than it does for someone else, but the principle is the same: the most valuable thing you have to offer is your time. Without it, nothing you choose to nurture can grow or flourish.

Your *attention* is the price you must pay. Without it, what you nurture cannot survive.

Consistency speaks louder than words. It strengthens, molds, and repeatedly communicates your intention to the recipient.

Nurture what you need.

Nurture what you love.

Nurture whatever has value and meaning to you.

Stop regretting what you should have done. Invest fully in the moments—birthdays, holidays, meet-ups for lunch, date nights, work meetings, or anything else that matters.

Because if it's important enough to regret later, it's important enough to nurture today.

Remember, tomorrow is a promise to no one.

DAILY AFFIRMATIONS:

"I choose to appreciate what I have, what is happening, and what has yet to come."

"Today is another chance to make the most of everything in all that I say and do."

"I honor this moment, receiving its gifts and releasing gratitude into the world."

"The Power of Why"

"We all make choices, but in the end, our choices make us." —Ken Levine

Decisions are an inevitable part of life.

You actually make thousands of choices every single day—it's estimated that the average person makes about 35,000 remotely conscious decisions each day.

While there's no bulletproof way to always make the right choice, there is one simple principle to live by that helps make a decision as sound and meaningful as it can be.

You have to be able to answer the question...

WHY?

Whatever you choose to do or not do, say or not say, feel or not feel, you've got to be able to answer that question.

Shrugging your shoulders is not an answer, and replying with "I don't know" or "I guess I wasn't thinking" just doesn't cut it.

That said, your answer may not be the best or proudest reason you've ever come up with.

But that's okay.

At least it's an answer that represents a step in the right direction, a step toward gaining clarity and reaching some sort of understanding.

Living your life according to this principle is a healthy measure of self-accountability.

It's a great way to get into the habit of thinking before you act or react.

Taking ownership of your feelings and claiming responsibility for your actions is the practice of discovering the answers that help address the question of "why."

Whether it be support and empathy or judgment and disdain, knowing the reason why quells the fires of speculation and gives rise to understanding even the unimaginable.

DAILY AFFIRMATIONS:

"I am making my choices consciously and with clarity, taking full responsibility for my actions."

"I pause, reflect, and answer 'why' before I act, creating a life of purpose and clarity."

"My why is my reason, not my excuse."

CHAPTER 7

Celebrating You

Every step you've taken is proof that change is possible—and that you are worthy of the benefits.

You've made it to this point and that's something.

In fact, it's everything.

Because no matter where you started or how tough it felt along the way, you stayed with it.

That alone shows there's a quiet strength in you that's not going anywhere.

You've made great decisions so far.

You chose this book.

You invested valuable time and energy in yourself.

You put in the work.

The momentum is in your favor.

While this is the final chapter of the book I'm sure you still have more to do, other things to work on.

That's completely normal.

Because change isn't about rushing; it's about rising moment by moment, reaching for something more, striving to do better and be better.

It's a process.

A process that takes time.

I know firsthand because I still follow through with my own private changing room ritual (every day) to this very day.

Once I started, l never stopped.

I never looked back.

It's brought me a sense of peace and contentment that I believe everyone should get the chance to experience and enjoy.

I want the same for you.

It's one of the reasons I wrote this book.

I wanted it to be a supportive guide as well as a continuous source of motivation and perspective, available right at your fingertips.

Hopefully it has served its purpose.

Just remember, if at any time you feel as though you could use more support, or need more clarity, or some personal guidance,

I'm here.

I am more than just an author, speaker, and coach.

I am a real person.

So I want you to know that my hand is extended and my door is always open.

In fact, I would love to hear from you.

You can connect with me online, inside the *Continue The Conversation* community by visiting **joegreenspeaks.com/Connect** or you can

Scan the QR code below.

The *Continue The Conversation Community* is a relaxed space designed for people like you who want to deepen their self-awareness, get ongoing motivation, explore new perspectives, and find more of what they personally need to make meaningful change really last.

You might enjoy reading some of the most recent weekly motivational *Action Quotes* or find interest in my *Dear Joe,* "**Words of Wisdom**" advice column.

There are free resources available for download such as the *"Change Your Mind, Change Their Mind"* worksheet and more.

I think you'll find that while the information is free, the benefits are priceless.

I'm not afraid to give away good stuff that really helps.

That's just good karma—and that's the vibe inside the *Continue The Conversation Community.*

No pressure.

Just possibilities.

With gratitude,

Joe Green

RESOURCES

"The Changing Room" **Workbook** is a source of motivation and guidance that becomes an instant journal and valuable blueprint for your own personal success.

Your Free *"Changing Room Starter Kit"* **joegreenspeaks.com/StarterKit**

Visit *"Continue The Conversation Community"* **joegreenspeaks.com/ Connect** A great source of continued motivation and guidance.

You might enjoy reading some of the most recent weekly motivational **Action Quotes** or find interest in the *Dear Joe, "Words of Wisdom" advice column.*

You will also find free resources you can download and use right now such as the *"Change Your Mind, Change Their Mind" worksheet* and more.

The *"Change of Life" Workshop* is also offered as a self-paced *course*.

www.ingramcontent.com/pod-product-compliance
Lightning Source LLC
Chambersburg PA
CBHW021136130626
46554CB00005B/1528